CLUB FED

The Good, the Bad, and the Fixable —
An Insider's View on the Federal Reserve

Club Fed

The Good, the Bad, and the Fixable
— An Insider's View on the Federal
Reserve

Toby Madden

Power Parametrics LLC

ISBN 978-0-9966186-0-1

Library of Congress Control Number: 2015911752

Tobias Madden
www.tobiasmadden.com
clubfedbook.com
powerparametrics.com

In memory of Frank T. Madden

CONTENTS

Foreword

"Money has never made man happy, nor will it, there is nothing in its nature to produce happiness. The more of it one has, the more one wants."

-Benjamin Franklin, Founding Father

Foreword

Money makes the world go around.

Money never sleeps.

Money is power.

Money is time.

Money talks.

Money is opportunity.

Money is the root of all evil.

Money is created by the *Federal Reserve.*

Foreword

I am an economist who worked at the Federal Reserve Bank of Minneapolis for twenty years. The Federal Reserve, or the Fed, is the central bank of the United States. The Fed is essentially independent, lacks *competitive* pressures, and provides a stimulating, collegial work environment. There are opportunities for Fed employees to do good.

I love the Fed because it greatly benefits America in a number of ways. It provides the country with an official *currency*, oversees the country's lending and banking system, and keeps *inflation* under control.

However, the Fed is not perfect. It creates a number of big problems for the United States of America. People who work for an organization that creates money can be blind to the damage it does.

I am writing this book because I love the Fed, want to see it improved, and want more people to understand what it is and what it does.

The ability to create money, the lack of competitive pressure, and the lack of outside oversight have created unnatural conditions in the Fed. Without economic constraints, three problems have surfaced at the Federal Reserve:

1.   It grossly overspends on its own operations.
2.   It does a poor job regulating banks.
3.   It increases wealth inequality.

As a free market economist, I am distraught at the severity of these problems. I propose simple solutions to these problems that are financially beneficial to all Americans.

Foreword

These solutions could be implemented without hampering the Fed's main objectives.

This book is organized into four parts:

Part I

Part I explains money, banking, and the Federal Reserve. There are numerous ways to create money. I provide examples of various monies used around the world, including Federal Reserve Notes, which are America's official currency. I also discuss the three primary functions of money and describe the other interesting forms money can take.

Banking is very important to society, but is inherently unstable. The Fed was created to increase stability. More detailed information on the history of banking and the Fed can be found in Appendix A.

Part II

The second part of this book deals with the "fatness" of the Fed. This section provides detailed examples of ways the Fed overindulges in its spending on niceties for employees. It describes the output that does not relate to the Fed's mission. Paradoxically, it also discusses the portions of the Fed that operate like they are in a competitive business environment. More examples of unrelated output can be found in Appendix B.

Part III

Foreword

The third part deals with the close relationship between banks and their regulators like the Fed. This section of the book describes the blunders that occur in the supervision and regulation of banks.

Part IV

The last part discusses how the Fed's *monetary policy* actions increase wealth inequality. The current monetary policy favors the rich. The solution to this problem can help you financially.

Knowledge of economic and financial concepts can help people make better decisions. Throughout this book, important concepts are *italicized*. Definitions of these concepts can be found in the glossary. If you read this book and understand the concepts presented, you will understand many of the fundamentals taught in *economics* and finance courses.

I have written in simple, straightforward language to make the concepts discussed in this book easy for someone without a background in economics to understand. In the process of simplifying, I removed many nuances of the material. Even so, my main points should still stand, and readers with a background in economics should find my conclusions provocative.

Economic concepts are very powerful, but can also be a curse. Unfortunately, after you learn a few of the main concepts of economics, you may find yourself distracted by the economic implications of everyday decisions, such as the concept of *opportunity cost*. Opportunity cost is whatever must be given up to obtain some item. It relates to the saying, "there is no such thing as a free lunch."

"Wait a minute," you may think, "somebody bought me lunch; I got a free lunch because it didn't *cost* me anything." Though you didn't pay any money for the meal, you experienced an opportunity cost. Even though someone paid for your lunch, you had to go to lunch, and listen to him or her talk all afternoon when you could have been doing something else. Instead of eating that free lunch, you could have been out swimming, playing tennis, or eating with somebody more interesting.

As an economist, I can tell you that the time you spend reading this book will be well worth the opportunity cost. This book will provide you with a better understanding of economics, finance, and the Fed.

Part I: Money, Banking, and the Federal Reserve

Chapter 1: Money is Power

"When I was young I thought that money was the most important thing in life; now that I am old, I know that it is."
-Oscar Wilde, Author

Part 1 – Money, Banking, and the Federal Reserve

What would you do if you could create *money* out of thin air? You would not have to tend to a "money tree" or pull money from its branches, you could simply create it. Would you spend it on prostitutes and cocaine, like the *Wolf of Wall Street*? Would you fund research to discover vaccines, like Bill Gates? Or would you be like my wife, a teacher, who would give schools the money to provide an additional teacher for every classroom?

When presented with this dilemma, different people have made different decisions. One *central bank* president used the power of money to influence politics across the country and tried to buy the U.S. presidency. To do this, he used the central bank to lend money to certain politicians. Additionally, he restricted loans to political enemies and certain geographic areas of the country to create *recessions* in these areas, so local politicians would be perceived negatively.

This central bank president thought his power was so immense that he could control the whole country, but the incumbent president saw through the evil use of money and refused to let the central bank re-charter in 1836. The name of this central bank president was Nicholas Biddle, the president of the Second Bank of the United States, and his efforts to financially support Henry Clay in the 1832 election failed when the American public re-elected President Andrew Jackson.[1] As a result, the United States did not have a central bank from 1836 until 1913.[2]

Chapter 1 – Money is Power

Sam Cash

You don't have to be an official central bank to create money and influence; anyone can make money, all that is needed are people who are willing to accept it. A few years ago, I met Sam Goaley and heard his story about how he created "Sam Cash." Sam was in second grade in South Saint Paul, Minnesota, when he started making this currency. Sam's money was nothing more than pieces of paper with numbers written on them.

Sam exchanged Sam Cash with his classmates for U.S. dollars. At first, his classmates used Sam Cash to purchase pencil toppers, the fad in their school at the time. Sam purchased the pencil toppers in bulk online. He used the pencil toppers as a standard to back his currency and was able to exchange his currency with other students at an *exchange rate* of 1 U.S. dollar for 5 Sam Cash. Sam wrote a "5" in each corner of a piece of paper, and Sam Cash was born. Sam received $1 in *seigniorage* for each 5 Sam Cash. There were roughly 1,000 Sam Cash in the initial *money supply*, distributed among about 20 people. In addition to pencil toppers, Sam's classmates began using the Sam Cash to purchase arts and crafts created by other students. Sam also set up a Blackjack casino where people could bet Sam Cash. Sam, as the dealer, could never run out of money, because if someone tried to "break the bank," he could just create more Sam Cash.

After about five months of creating money, Sam Cash began to experience *hyperinflation* as the dollar experienced high *appreciation* relative to Sam Cash. At one point, the exchange rate for U.S. Dollars was $1 per 1,000,000 Sam Cash. He *traded* Sam Cash at any rate his classmates were willing to pay, which contributed greatly to its hyperinflation. In his words, "we thought we could make more money by selling more, but then people would pay less for the Sam Cash." Asked about whether the early buyers of Sam Cash were upset about the inflation, Sam stated, "They kind of adapted to it. It's not like they really had a choice."

Other students in Sam's class tried to create their own forms of currency in order to compete with Sam Cash. To them, it was unfair that only one person was in charge of printing and distributing the currency. However, Sam Cash was so successful that Sam was able to buy out his competitors, establishing Sam Cash as the sole elementary school currency.

Classmates also attempted to counterfeit Sam Cash. The simple paper notes were easy to counterfeit, but after learning of the fraud, Sam began applying serial numbers to each bill, and fined the counterfeiters for "a lot" of Sam Cash.

As time went on, parents became more wary of their children's financial decisions, and they demanded that Sam's teacher shut down his currency business, referring to it as "Scam Cash." After a year and a half of supplying Sam Cash to his classmates, Sam Goaley's currency creation business came to an end. The now 15-year-old Sam Goaley aspires someday be an investment banker.

In many ways, what Sam did in second grade parallels what the Fed has done since its beginning. Both Sam and the Fed create money out of thin air. He also faced many of the same problems as has the Fed, such as inflation and counterfeits. Similarly, when inflation occurs in our economy, as it did in Sam's, we have to deal with it. We don't really have a choice.

When told the story of Sam Cash, Art Rolnick, a Senior Fellow at the University of Minnesota and former Federal Reserve Bank employee, said he thinks Sam Cash is an anomaly. Rolnick believes a currency is a *public good*, and that a private currency cannot survive.[3]

Academy of Finance

Money is a form of power, and Kris Sommerville figured out a way to harness this power. Kris Sommerville is the Academy of Finance Coordinator for Como Park Senior High School in St. Paul, Minnesota. The Academy of Finance is a program within the high school that allows students to study accounting, leadership, and other skills to prepare for college and a professional career. Essentially, the Academy of Finance seeks to teach high school students about business. In many high schools, business classes have been cut, and Kris was one of many concerned educators who felt that students were not being properly prepared to work or study in a professional environment. Students at the Academy of Finance receive college credit for business courses through a local community college. They also have the opportunity to participate in an internship in their junior and senior years. Kris created Academy of Finance bucks (AoF bucks) to motivate her students. AoF bucks act as a reward system. When students do something above and beyond what is expected of them, they are rewarded with this money. Kris acknowledges that many teachers have similar *incentive* programs. As part of the Academy of Finance, she thinks using AoF bucks makes a lot of sense because it teaches kids even more about money and finance. They get paid for their behavior, as they would in a job.

The students can use AoF bucks to buy food and prizes. Some students spend their bucks as soon as they get them, and others save them. Some students save for big prizes, but Kris says others don't really have a reason for saving their bucks. She thinks some save because "they just like the cushion." This creates a sort of wealth inequality, and Kris explains that there isn't really a "middle class."

Beyond spending, the students can invest the bucks in a program run by an AoF credit union. The students can deposit their money and earn *interest* on it, receiving back more money than they deposited. The bank also has incentives to deposit more of your money. If you bring in 15 AoF bucks for deposit, the bank waives the 5 AoF bucks fee for starting an account. The credit union does not yet provide loans, but Kris believes that this is an addition that would teach kids even more about understanding money and banking.

Trading among the kids began to occur as well. Kris doesn't mind this because she believes it mirrors real life. Fortunately, unlike the world of Sam Cash, no counterfeits were created and no one created a competing currency.

The exchange rate between AoF bucks and U.S. dollars would fluctuate between about 1:1 and 2:1. Inflation didn't necessarily occur in a big way. However, certain teachers were more willing to give out the bucks than were others and some would charge more for rewards than others. This appeared unfair to a lot of kids, but Kris explained to the students that this is how it would work in real life. Some employers pay more than others, and some businesses charge more for certain goods than others. However, teachers at the Academy of Finance do not face *competition*. Students do not have the freedom to leave one teacher if they don't pay enough, or if they charge too much.

This also means that the AoF bucks aren't very consistent and metered. In the next school year, Kris plans to streamline the system. For example, instead of being rewarded for doing something good, which is very subjective, students will be rewarded for things like their grades, making the system work more like receiving a paycheck.

With the AoF bucks incentive system, Kris is able to motivate her students to participate and perform better in school. She teaches them valuable real-world lessons about money and finance.

The Three Functions of Money

Like the currencies described above, all money must have three major functions in order to be successful. Money's three functions are to serve as a medium of exchange, a unit of account, and a store of value[4]. These three functions can be used to evaluate the many forms of money in the world.

Medium of Exchange

A medium of exchange is something that can be used to transfer value between people. A one-dollar bill, more formally known as a one-dollar Federal Reserve Note, is easily given to a shopkeeper for a pack of gum. If you didn't have one dollar, you could also give the shopkeeper four quarters, or a five-dollar bill, in exchange for the gum and four ones. Almost everyone recognizes the value of U.S. currency, which makes it easy to trade. This ease of transaction makes currency and coins a good medium of exchange.

Unit of Account

A unit of account is something that can be used to measure the value of things. U.S. currency is a common standard used to measure the worth of something. For example, the price of a pack of gum is about $1 at most stores. The value of a U.S. dollar is fairly consistent and widely accepted, which makes it a good tool to measure value.

Store of Value

Serving as a store of value means that the value of this money today is pretty much what the value of the money will be in the future. This means that money or any other *commodity* may be kept over periods of time and exchanged for goods of a similar value in the future.

Examples of Money

Anything can be used as money, and a money's effectiveness can be gauged by these three functions. For example, the chair in which you are sitting could be used as money. You could measure things in terms of chairs – I owe you 3 chairs, or I owe you one seat and four legs. Chairs have a pretty good store of value – they are sturdy and should last a long time. However, as a medium of exchange, chairs are not very good money. Imagine trying to give someone a payment of ten chairs – you could hurt your back in the transaction.

The people of Yap once used big stones as money.[5] This money faces some of the same problems that chairs face. Many different types of money, other than paper currency, have been used throughout history. Think of cigarettes in prison or during war time. I could owe you a half pack of cigarettes, or maybe two packs, or a carton, illustrating another good medium of exchange. Cigarettes are also a good unit of account and serve as a decent store of value.

Previously used monies were mainly *commodity money*, money that takes the form of a commodity with intrinsic value. Gold coins are an example. Here are some other examples of previously used commodity monies:

- **Livestock**: During the agricultural revolution, forms of livestock – such as cows, sheep, and cattle – served as early money in many cultures. Grain and other vegetables were also used as money.[6]

- **Wampum**: Wampum was first used as money by the Narragansett tribe of Rhode Island. Roughly translated as "white shell beads," Wampum was initially exchanged between members of the Narragansett tribe during tribal ceremonies. After the European settlers arrived in New England, they exploited Wampum to gain power and territory from the Narragansett tribe members.[7]
- **Cowrie Shells**: Cowries are sea snails from the Pacific and Indian Oceans. Their ornate shells were used as currencies as recently as the 20th century in many African, Asian, and Native American cultures.[8]
- **Salt**: In many cultures of the ancient world, salt was valued in weight on par with gold.[9]
- **Cacao Beans**: An important commodity in early Central America, cacao beans was used to make liquid chocolate for royal and religious ceremonies. Sales of a bundle of cacao, each holding 24,000 beans, served as money.[10]

Bitcoin

Cryptocurrencies are an interesting and relatively new form of money. Bitcoin is one of the most popular cryptocurrencies. It only exists online; bitcoin transactions are similar to online credit card transactions. The appeal of bitcoin is that users can exchange currency safely without using banks; transactions are monitored by other bitcoin users, rather than by banks. Those who use their own computers to supervise transactions are rewarded with bitcoin. This allows transactions to occur without the involvement of a bank or credit card company. The aim of bitcoin is to make trading money easier and to limit the role of governments and banks in the exchange of currency.

How does Bitcoin rate as money when compared against money's three functions? Because it is virtual, it is a good unit of account. The value of something can be easily measured in bitcoin or fractions of a bitcoin.

However, bitcoin doesn't serve as well as a medium of exchange. At first, bitcoin could only be exchanged among users online, but more and more businesses, such as Expedia and overstock.com, have begun to accept bitcoin.[11] Even as more *institutions* allow you to spend bitcoin, it is still very difficult to obtain and store the currency. The complexity of the system limits its user-friendliness.

Today, new bitcoin is created and given as payment to those who monitor transactions, but according to the founders of the currency, no more than 21 million bitcoin will be created.[12] When this limit is reached, those who monitor transactions will collect small transaction fees, like a bank.

The limit of bitcoin acts to prevent inflation, strengthening bitcoin use as a store of value. However, its value has been very volatile. There are huge fluctuations in the value of bitcoin compared to other currencies (see chart 1). This money is still in its infancy, and complex *markets* for the bitcoin, such as futures and options, have yet to develop.

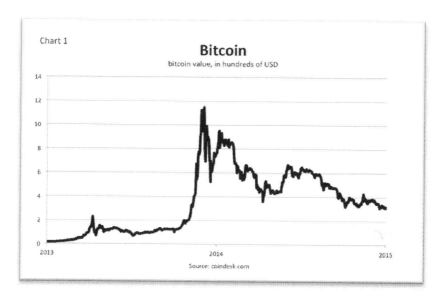

Chart 1

Bitcoin

bitcoin value, in hundreds of USD

Source: coindesk.com

Fiat Money vs. Specie Money

Fiat money is a system of money that is backed by government regulation or law, rather than a physical commodity. Fiat money is based on the relationship between *supply and demand*, rather than the value of what the money is made. In essence, fiat money is based on faith.

Before fiat money, there was *specie money*. Specie money is backed by some type of metal, such as gold or silver. For a long part of its history, the United States currency was a specie money backed by gold.

There has been a lot of debate about whether the *gold standard* is better than fiat currency. The advantage of a currency backed by gold is that over a long period of time the value of the currency remains about the same. However, in the

13

short run, the value of gold can vary tremendously. In times where new gold mines are exploited, the amount of money in circulation expands, causing inflation. At other times, when the economy expands, deflation occurs. The value of a specie currency varies widely year-to-year, but remains relatively stable over time.

On the other hand, the value of fiat currency remains relatively stable in the short-term, but typically experiences inflation over time: 5.4 cents in 1933 carried the same value as 1 dollar in 2015. Thus, 1 dollar in the 1933 economy would be the equivalent of almost 19 dollars in today's economy.

In 1933, the United States went off the gold standard and started using a fiat currency. Chart 2 displays changes in short-term prices, shown by the inflation rate and in long-term prices, shown by the consumer price index. The chart demonstrates that when the U.S. switched from a specie currency to a fiat currency, short-term prices stabilized, but long-term prices began to increase steadily.

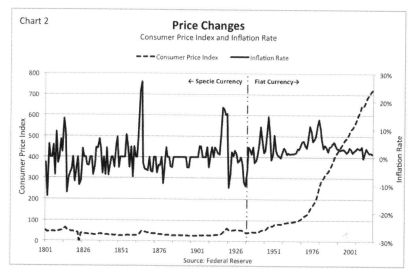

Federal Reserve Notes

Central banks around the world create money with the push of a button. For instance, the Fed, the central bank of the United States, creates the United States' currency: the Federal Reserve Note. Reach in your pocket right now and pull out one of those green pieces of paper that you have been carrying around. Notice that "Federal Reserve Note" is printed on the front of the note at the top. Also note the words, "this note is legal tender for all debts public and private."

This note was printed by one of the two plants operated by the U.S. Treasury's Bureau of Engraving and Printing, located in Washington DC and Fort Worth, Texas. Look in the lower right quadrant of the note and you will find a small letter with an even smaller number next to it. If the note was printed in Fort Worth, there will be an "FW" next to the small letter.

15

Bills printed in Washington D.C. do not have anything printed next to the small letter.

The U.S. dollar is a fiat currency, meaning that a dollar has no intrinsic value, but is used as money because of government decree.

Besides notes, money can also come in the form of coins. Coins are created in mints. There are several mints in the United States. The largest and oldest mint is in Philadelphia, which dates back to 1792 when Philadelphia was the capital of the United States.[13] There are also mints in Denver and San Francisco, created during the height of each region's respective gold rush. The newest, smallest mint is in West Point, New York. Each mint engraves its coin with a stamp bearing the first letter of the mint in which the coin was produced (P, D, S, and W, respectively).[14]

When economists discuss the country's money supply, they use two primary categorizations. *M1* refers to all paper currency and coin, as well as all money in checking accounts. *M2* is a slightly broader category, which includes M1 currency in addition to the balances of all savings accounts and money market funds.

U.S. dollars appear to be "good" money when considering the three purposes of money. In fact, the dollar is used in place of some other countries' "bad" money, including Ecuador and El Salvador.[15] The central banks of Ecuador and El Salvador created too much inflation, so their currencies were not a very good store of value. The United States benefits from additional seigniorage from other countries' use of Federal Reserve Notes because it only costs a few cents to make a Federal Reserve Note, but the Fed trades them at full face value. When there are more U.S. dollars in circulation, the Fed earns more seigniorage.

Hyperinflation

There have been numerous episodes of fiat currencies losing most of their value. The dramatic loss of a currency's value is called hyperinflation. A few episodes in the United States include the Revolutionary continentals, or the Civil War "greenbacks."

Hyperinflation occurred in Germany in the early 1920s when most of the printing presses in the country were creating German marks. It is interesting to see German marks before and after the hyperinflation. The mark note of 1920 was a work of art, beautifully engraved on both sides of sturdy paper with awesome depictions of life. In contrast, the 50 billion mark note of 1923 was printed with just characters on one side, using very cheap paper and ink.

The use of these massive numbers in daily transactions by German citizens warped their thinking and sometimes caused psychosis.[16] Zero stroke was a mental condition noted by doctors in the Weimar Republic, brought on by the huge calculations necessary to carry out everyday transactions. Zero stroke manifested itself as a compulsion to write endless strings of zeroes and a confusion about simple numbers. For example, patients said they were 45 billion years old or that they had 2 trillion kids. Bankers, bookkeepers, and cashiers were the most prone to this illness due to their professions requiring lengthy calculations.

Chapter 1 – Money is Power

Because unpredictable changes in price can strain an economy, it is very important that central banks keep the value of money constant so that it can serve as an effective "store of value." History has shown that countries with independent central banks have lower levels of inflation, and banks that are influenced by politics face greater inflation. For example, the Central Bank of Argentina's mandate was rephrased in 2012 to subject it to a greater amount of political influence.[17] In response, inflation increased. The value of the Argentine peso fell by more than 50 percent between 2012 and 2015.[18]

Politicians have incentives to push the central bank to print more money in order to get re-elected. When people have more money in their pockets, they tend to vote in favor of the incumbent. However, printing more money can increase inflation over time.

That is why the U.S. Congress insists that the Fed's monetary policy strive for low and stable prices. Fortunately, the leaders of the Fed, the Board of Governors, have a 14-year term.[19] A 14-year term reduces the pressure for governors to please politicians in order to get re-elected. Because governors do not need to worry about reelection, their actions are less likely to be swayed by politicians. Thus, they can concentrate on their twin objectives of promoting *full employment* and low inflation.[20] Full employment is a notable goal because unemployed people are not producing for society or themselves. *Unemployment insurance* is available so unemployed people are not forced to take inferior jobs, yet it costs firms a lot of money. However, the Fed's independence and ability to create money have the unfortunate consequence of sacrificing the *efficiency* of the Fed's operations. There are no *taxes* to raise, competition to deal with, or customers to serve.

Art Rolnick agrees that the Fed doesn't exactly face competition. The Fed "has a *monopoly* on issuing money," he said. On the other hand, Rolnick pointed out that the Fed must report to Congress regularly.[21] More information about the Fed's oversight is contained in Chapter 3.

Money is closely aligned with the banking system. Banks lend out money and also create additional money through the *fractional reserve banking system*, which is discussed at length in the next chapter.

Chapter 2: Banking is Always Unstable

"I sincerely believe... that banking establishments are more dangerous than standing armies."
-Thomas Jefferson, President

The very nature of banking is unstable. This instability has caused bank panics and recessions. The causes of this instability are twofold: the use of other people's money and the fractional banking system.

Other People's Money

When you own a bank, you invest a little and borrow a lot. This gives you the *incentive* to take on risk. Here's an example:

You have $1,000 to invest in something. So you decide to create two banks, Red Bank and Black Bank, by investing $500 in each. Each bank then takes in $4,500 in deposits. So each bank has $5,000 in cash (your investment of $500 and $4,500 of other people's money.) Because you own both banks, you decide how each bank should invest.

In this situation, you could safely invest by betting it on a game of Roulette.

Roulette is a casino game that has a wheel with 37 pockets on it. The wheel spins, and a ball is released and eventually lands in one of the 37 pockets. Eighteen pockets are red and eighteen pockets are black. In real roulette, there is one green pocket, but we will ignore this to simplify the example.

Half of the time, the ball rests in a red pocket, the other half, it rests in a black pocket. If you place a bet on a color and the ball lands in a pocket of that color, your prize is double your bet.

Chapter 2 – Banking is Always Unstable

Red Bank bets $5,000 on red and Black Bank bets $5,000 on black on the same Roulette spin. One bank will lose and the other bank will win. Let's say the ball rolls into a red pocket. Red Bank is very happy! It now has $10,000. Black Bank is sad because it now has nothing.

What happens next? Black Bank reports to its depositors that unfortunately, the bank made a bad investment and lost their $4,500 in deposits, as well as the $500 investment. Sorry depositors, Black Bank is shutting down.

Meanwhile, Red Bank reports record earnings and has $10,000 cash. They decide to return the depositors' $4,500 in deposits plus a little interest. Red Bank is left with $5,500 in cash minus the interest paid to depositors. Before paying interest, your initial $1,000 investment has grown to $5,500. You just made four and half times your initial investment of $1,000 in one fun trip to Vegas!

Other people's money is great!

Unless you are the other person.

If you are the other person, you could study the bank's management and financial statements, to see if it is a good investment. But is it really worth your time (remember opportunity costs) to do all the work of analyzing the bank's creditworthiness? Probably not, especially if you are only depositing a small amount. You look at the huge bank building, made of solid marble, and the workers inside dressed in fancy suits, and think: "this bank is solid as a rock."

22

Even with the rock solid appearance, all banks have an incentive to take risks because they are using other people's money. They may not go to Vegas, but they have an incentive to make riskier loans with higher interest rates.

Risk-taking increases when the *capital ratio* is small. The bank owners invest their money in ownership. This is their "skin in the game" and can have many names such as *equity* or *capital*.

Assets are things that have value, like buildings, cars and cash. In the above example, each bank started with $5,000 in cash, ($500 in capital and $4,500 in customer deposits) which are the bank's only assets. Their capital ratio was 10 percent ($500 in capital / $5,000 in assets). Their capital ratio would decrease if they increased the deposits taken in but did not increase their ownership investment. If they took in $9,500 in deposits and had $500 invested in capital, the capital ratio would decrease to 5 percent ($500 capital / $10,000 cash). The opposite of an asset is a *liability*. A liability holds negative value, usually a debt that needs to be paid, i.e., a mortgage or a credit card bill.

Banking assets consist of loans, investments, and cash. Liabilities include deposits such as savings accounts, checking accounts, and certificates of deposit. *Bonds* are another liability owned by some commercial banks.

To counteract the risk-taking by banks, governments have put rules and regulations in place. These rules and regulations require banks to hold a certain amount of capital, to hold cash in reserve in their vaults, and to diversify their loans to different industries, geographic areas, and customers.

Even with these rules and regulations, banks still have an incentive to take on risk. Incentives do matter. In part III, you will find examples where banks took excessive risk and got away with it.

Fractional Reserve Banking and Money Creation

Banks are also inherently unstable because they only hold a fraction of the money received in deposits as cash in their vaults. This is called *fractional reserve banking*. The amount of money that they are required to hold in reserve in their vaults is called the *reserve requirement*.

The fractional banking system creates money in society. Money includes not only currency and coins, but also the balances in people's checking and savings accounts.

The money not held in reserve in the bank's vault is lent out to people who borrow from the bank. Banks get revenues by charging interest and fees on the loans that they make. Banks' expenses include management costs and the interest paid on deposits.

The act of lending by banks in the fractional system creates additional money. For example, if you deposit $100 into your checking account, and your bank is required to hold onto $10 in *reserves*; they can lend out $90. The person who borrowed the $90 usually deposits it into his or her checking account. Now, that bank has an additional $90, and is required to keep 10 percent of that, or $9. Therefore it can lend out $81. The person who receives $81 deposits it into his or her checking account. Just these three iterations create $271 ($100

+ \$90 + \$81). These iterations will go on and on to create money through the lending process.

The total amount of money created can be calculated by the *money multiplier*. The money multiplier equals one divided by the reserve requirement. So, if the reserve requirement is 10 percent, the money multiplier equals 1/10 percent = 1/0.1 which equals 10.

With a money multiplier of 10, a deposit of \$100 turns into \$1,000. On the other hand, if the person withdraws his or her original one hundred dollars, then through the money multiplier working in reverse, \$1,000 disappears.

In the fractional banking system, the instability occurs due to a tendency toward booms and busts. When more lending occurs, the overall economy booms. People who borrow often invest in physical things like homes, cars, stores, and factories. However, if a lot of people withdraw cash, the bank can quickly get low on currency. When someone tries to take out money and the bank is out of cash, people start to panic, and this causes a bank panic. Such a panic occurs in the fictional movie *It's a Wonderful Life*.[22] We all feel for George Bailey as he tries to explain the fractional banking system to the customers. He doesn't have their deposits because the neighbor borrowed it to buy a house.

The practice of fractional reserve banking has not always been used. Often, the practice is criticized for creating instability. Recent instability in Iceland's economy has caused the government to consider discarding the fractional reserve system for a *full reserve system*, which would disallow the practice of lending other people's money while keeping it available for withdrawal. Instead, the depositor would hold time deposits and *demand deposits*. Demand deposits work just like a checking account in a fractional reserve system, but he bank is required to hold 100 percent of demand deposits, effectively setting the money multiplier at one. Funds from the time deposit accounts could be lent out, but would not be available to the original depositor for the duration of the loan.

Following the financial crisis, the Prime Minister of Iceland commissioned a study to determine the best way to change the country's monetary system. The report, released in April 2015, recommended that the country adopt a full reserve banking system.[23]

Bank Panics

Most banking panics in the United States occurred in the 1800s, when people became nervous that their banks were becoming insolvent and rushed to withdraw their money as soon as they could, causing banks to call their loans back. In other words, if you had a loan from a bank that wasn't doing well, it would come to you and say, "We want our money back." This puts a big damper on economic activity because there is a reduction in lending, thus a reduction in investment, infrastructure, and equipment, which can cause recessions.

The boom-bust cycles of the 1800s were severe. When people had faith in the banking industry, banks tended to be very generous with loans and people were eager to invest. Banks tried to portray an image of solid financial footing by building large stone structures to give comfort to depositors.

Both banks and people tended to overextend themselves. People borrowed too much, and banks lent too much. This phenomenon is known as the boom part of the cycle. When people discovered banks were lending out such significant amounts of money, they became concerned, wondering if they would be able to get their deposits back from the banks. Panic ensued as people rushed to the banks to get their money back. This is the bust part of the cycle. Banks had lent out the deposited money as loans, and couldn't give every customer back his or her full deposit. Because of this, banks would have to close down, causing even more panic, and ultimately recession or *depression* in the economy.

A particularly bad banking bust happened in 1907 in New York. As a result, the country and economy suffered.

However, J.P. Morgan, the wealthiest banker in New York at the time, was able to rally together other New York bankers in order to form a "money trust," which served as a lender of last resort to the failing banks, allowing them to recover from the crisis. Big names like John D. Rockefeller (the wealthiest man in the country) and George B. Cortelyou (the U.S. Secretary of the Treasury at the time) worked to restore confidence in the banks. This allowed the nation's economy to recover.[24]

However, it wasn't long until citizens began to fear that Morgan's ability completely to refund the banks implied that the United States was becoming a plutocracy, a country completely controlled by the rich. Thus, Louisiana house representative Arsène Pujo, the chair of the House Committee on Banking and Currency, created the Pujo Committee to investigate J.P. Morgan and other prominent bankers in the "money trust." The public's skepticism of the rich influenced Congress to write the Federal Reserve Act, which was signed by President Woodrow Wilson on December 23, 1913.[25]

The Fed's primary goal at its inception was to serve as a lender of last resort, according to Art Rolnick. The Fed was essentially created to keep America's banking industry stable. It wasn't until later that the Fed adopted other goals, like monetary policy.[26]

Chapter 3: The Federal Reserve Creates Stability

"Now it's solid
Solid as a rock
That's what this love is
That's what we've got."

Lyrics from "Solid" by Ashford & Simpson

This chapter briefly explains the history and structure of central banking in the United States, a more thorough discussion is contained in Appendix A.

Chapter 3 – The Federal Reserve Creates Stability

Bank panics wreaked havoc in the United States, causing President Wilson to sign the Federal Reserve Act, officially creating the Fed.[27]

Wary of the concentration of too much power, and remembering Biddle's attempt to control the politics of the country through a central bank, Congress made the Fed decentralized. Can an institution be central and decentralized? In the case of the Fed, it can. To be central, the Board of Governors represents the interests of the Federal Government. To be decentralized, each regional bank represents the private interests of its region.

The Fed acts as a bankers' bank. Member banks are required to own stock in the Fed and have savings accounts with the Fed known as reserve accounts. As previously discussed, the Fed also acts as the sole producer of legal tender.

The Fed creates stability by reducing the risk of a bank panic. If a member bank is running low on cash, it sends its armored car to a Fed location to get more. Fed branches have huge vaults containing billions of dollars in currency, which the Fed uses to supply banks with cash.

Federal Reserve Structure

The *Federal Reserve System* is an organization of 12 Regional District Banks in Boston, New York, Philadelphia, Cleveland, Richmond, Atlanta, Chicago, St. Louis, Minneapolis, Kansas City, Dallas, and San Francisco. (See map)

Map of the Federal Reserve Districts

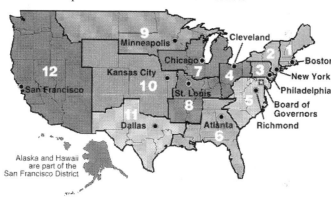

Source: Federal Reserve[28]

The 12 District Banks around the country are presided over by a Board of Governors in Washington, DC. The Governors serve 14-year terms and are nominated by the President of the United States and approved by Congress.

The Board of Governors is overseen by a Chairperson and Vice Chairperson, who are also nominated by the President and approved by the Senate.

For more information on the structure of the Federal Reserve, please see Appendix A.

31

The Fed has survived 100 years as an independent government agency. Even with the Great Depression and the recent financial collapse, the financial system has become more stable because of the Fed. This can be seen by the fact that banking crises have become much less common since the Federal Reserve Act.

Federal Reserve Responsibilities

Over time, the Fed has evolved to take on more responsibilities. Today, the Fed's duties fall into four general areas:

1) Providing financial services to depository institutions, the U.S. government, and foreign official institutions. The Fed plays a major role in operating the nation's payments system. Providing payment systems includes processing checks, facilitating electronic transactions, and making sure that banks have enough coin and currency.

2) Supervising and regulating banking institutions to ensure the safety and soundness of the nation's banking and financial system, and to protect the credit rights of consumers. In other words, the Fed is charged with making sure that banks are following the rules and are financially safe and healthy.

3) Maintaining the stability of the financial system and containing systemic risk that may arise in financial markets.

4) Conducting the nation's monetary policy by influencing the monetary and credit conditions in the economy in pursuit of maximum employment, stable prices, and moderate long-term interest rates. Monetary policy is one of the main objectives of the Fed; it is probably the most well-known and arguably the most important.[29]

Payment Systems

I was first hired at the Minneapolis Fed in 1995 as an analyst in the Automated Clearing House division (ACH). ACH is an electronic network for deposits and withdrawals. Think of getting your pay directly deposited into your account (and withdrawn from your employer's) or paying your electric bill online by having the money automatically withdrawn from your bank account and deposited into the utility company's account. The Fed's ACH area handles the transfer between accounts.

The ACH area, like most of the payment services provided by the Fed, is a "Priced Service." Priced services are the services that the Fed provides to member banks and charges them for. The cost per transaction can be as low as a fraction of a penny. Other priced services to banks include check processing, wire transfers, and settlement services.

These services may also be provided by private-sector operators. These private companies compete with the Fed in an *oligopoly*. As competitors, they are concerned with unfair competition because the Fed creates money out of thin air and therefore could subsidize the production of these services.

Congress addressed this problem with the Monetary Control Act of 1980. This law requires the Fed to recoup costs of "priced services" and make a normal *profit*. The revenue collected must be higher than the costs incurred in providing the services.

For these services, the Fed needs to act like a business. It has customers who pay for a service and the revenues collected have to exceed the expenses. The work environment at the Priced Services division of the Fed is very business-like. It focuses on providing excellent service and containing costs. This is why I was hired. My career to this point had been focused on making operations more efficient and I was asked to reduce resource use and contain costs. I had to create enough savings in this division to cover my salary and benefit expenses, otherwise I would get fired. Fortunately, I found enough savings in a more efficient use of computers.

The priced services area of the Fed is very efficient and effective. Because of competition, these areas are very lean and mean. Employees in the priced services area take only short breaks and sometimes complain of "sweatshop" conditions.

Art Rolnick believes that check processing is different from some of the other objectives of the Fed. He said the Fed could get out of managing payment systems and leave it to the private sector. On the other hand, he thinks monetary policy and currency management are tasks that can only be handled by a central bank.[30]

The other areas of the Fed are not so efficient. This costs you and the U.S. government money. This will be explained more in Part II - Fat Fed.

Supervision and Regulation of Banks

In addition to providing services to banks, the Fed regulates and examines them. As stated in the second chapter, banks are unstable and therefore highly regulated. One major responsibility of the Fed is to ensure the safety and soundness of financial institutions.

The Fed regulates bank holding companies, subsidiaries of bank holding companies, state member banks, and representative offices of foreign banks. It also works in conjunction with the *Federal Deposit Insurance Corporation* (FDIC) and the Office of the Comptroller of the Currency (OCC) to regulate banks.

The Fed is the sole regulator and supervisor of bank holding companies, which makes the Fed a dominant financial institution regulator. The Dodd Frank Act expanded the Fed's regulatory and supervisory responsibilities by requiring it to oversee large non-bank financial institutions that pose a systemic risk to the economy[31]. The Fed also works with state banking departments in supervising banks.

The Fed examines banks to ensure they are following the rules and also to check their financial health. Standard financial analysis for any organization falls into three intertwined concepts of solvency, profitability, and liquidity.

Solvency - Solvency is the ability of an organization to meet its financial obligations. Solvency is measured in equity, which is equal to assets minus liabilities. Because assets and liabilities can change over time, equity is measured at a certain point in time, usually the last day of a month or year. If a firm has positive equity, it is financially solvent. In other words, its assets are more valuable than its liabilities.

Profitability - *Profit* is revenue minus expenses. That is, how much you earn minus how much you spend. If you make more than you spend, you have a profit. If you spend more than you make, you have a loss. While equity is measured at a point in time, profits are measured over a period of time. Profits flow into your equity.

Liquidity - Liquidity is essentially the flexibility of assets. Even if a company or a person is financially solvent and profitable, they may struggle to meet financial obligations because assets such as property, equipment, and accounts receivable can't be used to repay debts, and can be difficult to convert to cash. If your assets are liquid, you have enough cash on hand to meet your short-term needs. Liquidity is measured at a specific point in time.

The Fed examines the financial health of banks using seven standards represented by the acronym "CAMELSS." These standards are:

- Capital: Does the bank have adequate capital? Do the owners have enough "skin in the game?"
- Assets: What is the quality of the bank's assets? Is it making good loans? Are the assets concentrated into a few areas or well diversified?
- Management: How strong is the bank's management? Does it have experience? Will it do a good job? Is it going to Vegas to bet the bank's assets?
- Earnings or profits: How much money does the bank make?
- Liquidity: Do the banks have enough cash to meet their short-term needs?
- Sensitivity: How sensitive is each bank to market risk and especially interest rate changes?
- Systemic risk: Is the bank a *systemically important institution*? An institution is systemically important if the Financial Stability Oversight Council determines that the failure of, or a disruption to the functioning of the institution could create or increase the risk of significant liquidity or credit problems spreading among financial institutions or markets and thereby threaten the stability of the U.S. financial system.[32]

Banks are rated on an overall scale of 1 to 5. The safest banks are rated 1 and the riskiest are rated 5. The banks are given a rating in each of the seven CAMELSS standards. Banks with high ratings are more closely scrutinized. These ratings and other information from the examinations are confidential to prevent runs on weaker banks. However, the rating history can be made public if a bank is shut down.

The Fed's bank examiners are housed in each of the 12 districts, but are overseen by the Fed's Board of Governors.

In addition to payment systems and banking supervision and regulation, the Fed also provides monetary policy.

Monetary Policy

Monetary policy is basically the creation or destruction of money. The Fed uses monetary policy to influence the economy and inflation. In order to accomplish this, the *Federal Open Market Committee* (FOMC) decides the direction of monetary policy. The FOMC is made up of 7 members of the Board of Governors and the 12 District bank presidents; however, there are only 12 voting members: 7 of the members are the Board of Governors in Washington D.C., the eighth member is the president of the Federal Reserve Bank of New York, and four of the remaining eleven District bank presidents serve one-year terms on a rotating basis.[33]

The Fed traditionally conducted monetary policy with the focus on price stability. However, in 1977 Congress directed the Fed to conduct monetary policy in pursuit of maximum employment, stable prices, and moderate long-term interest rates. This "dual mandate" created a controversy among economists.[34] Nobel Prize-winning economist Ed Prescott describes these goals as vague and difficult to follow.

Prescott does not like the goal of promoting full employment. "We wish we could do something about employment," he said.[35] He thinks that by setting this target, the Fed is promising to do something it cannot do.

The Fed has several tools to affect the money supply:

- *Open Market Operations* - The purchase and sale of government bonds. Open Market Operations are the most common tool used to affect the money supply.
- Reserve Requirement - Earlier we discussed that banks must hold a minimum amount of reserves for their deposits. The Fed has the power to change the reserve requirement. If the reserve requirement is low, then banks are capable of lending out more money, which increases the money supply.
- Interest on Reserves - The Fed has the power to pay interest to banks for holding reserves at the Fed. Paying more interest increases incentives for banks to hold reserves with the Fed and decreases incentives to lend out money to bank borrowers.
- *Discount Rate* - Rate of interest for banks to borrow from the Fed. When the discount rate is low, banks have more incentive to borrow from the Fed and make more loans, which increases the money supply.

The Fed's primary method to affect the money supply is Open Market Operations. By purchasing government bonds, the Fed pushes money into the system, increasing the money supply. Conversely, when the Fed sells government bonds, it takes money out of circulation, decreasing the money supply. The Open Market Operations desk at the Federal Reserve Bank of New York is most often in charge of these transactions.

When the Fed chooses to increase the money supply, it buys government bonds, or securities. It buys the securities through primary dealers, which are most often large Wall Street firms. These securities can be owned by individuals or corporations. The Open Market Operations desk makes an order to purchase these government securities and receives them from the primary dealer. The primary dealer's accounts with the Fed are credited, and the dealer then credits the accounts of their customers who own those bonds. In essence, the Fed purchases government securities from individuals and corporations, giving them more money in their bank accounts, which increases the money supply.

You may have heard of the term *quantitative easing*. This is a term used when the Fed uses Open Market Operations to purchase securities while short-term interest rates are near zero.

When the Fed wants to decrease the money supply, it simply does the opposite, selling bonds to dealers, holding onto money from the sales, and thereby removing the money from the money supply.

The reserve requirement is another tool the Fed can use to increase or decrease the money supply. If the Fed decides to change the reserve requirement, it can change it from, for example, 10 percent to 20 percent. What that means is if somebody deposits $100, then the bank is now required to hold onto $20 (20 percent) instead of the $10 (10 percent) of the deposit in its bank vault or with the Fed. This reduces the money multiplier, which means the bank has less money to lend out.

The Fed can also change the discount rate, which is the rate the Fed charges banks when it loans to them. When the discount rate is higher, lending becomes more expensive and banks become stricter about extending credit.

The Fed's monetary policy actions directly affect interest rates and inflation, and indirectly affect employment through changes in overall demand. If interest rates rise, then generally there will be less borrowing by the *law of demand.* The reduction in borrowing will reduce both overall demand and supply. A reduction in demand as well as supply will induce lower overall economic activity. If overall economic activity decreases, employment will decrease. The reverse happens when interest rates decrease.

If the Fed increases the money supply, more funds are available for lending and interest rates fall. If the Fed reduces the supply of money, there are fewer funds available for loans and interest rates rise.

The Fed's monetary policy actions target only certain interest rates, but all interest rates are affected with varying degrees of intensity. The effect of monetary policy directly impacts the risk-free interest rates and inflation premiums to interest rates. These are explained in the next section.

Interest Rates

When a bank or other lender makes a loan, it charges borrowers a fee called interest. An interest rate is the rate of interest charged on the principal (amount owed) over a period of time and is usually expressed as a percent.

To demonstrate interest rates, suppose you lend your friend $100 with the understanding that she will pay you $105 in one year. The extra $5 she pays back is called interest and the simple interest rate is 5 percent ($5 interest divided by $100 principle is 5 percent).

There are many types of loans, such as personal loans, home loans, car loans, credit card loans, certificates of deposit, and numerous more. Each type of loan can have a different length of time to be paid, different chance of being paid, and many other attributes. Because there are so many types of loans, there are many different interest rates.

If lenders take on more risk, they want to be compensated with a higher interest rate. There are numerous forms of risk, including time risk, inflation risk, credit risk, liquidity risk, exchange rate risk, and others.

Each one of these risks causes a premium to be added to a base interest rate.

- Risk-free rate - This is the base rate, sometimes called the real rate. An example of a risk-free rate is a United States Treasury bill that is payable tomorrow. The United States is one of a few countries that has always paid its debts. This rate is affected by the overall supply of savings and demand for funds, which are affected by the Fed's actions.
- Time premium - This premium is added on for loans that are longer that one day in duration. This differs based on when the loan is due.

- Inflation premium - Because inflation affects the *future value* of money, the anticipated inflation is added as a premium.

- Credit premium - The probability that the loan will not be paid back in full. This premium is affected by the amount and quality of *collateral*.
- Liquidity premium - The premium added when there are not a lot of willing buyers or sellers of a loan.
- Exchange rate premium - If the loan is denominated in another currency, a premium is added because of the risk of changes in exchange rates.
- Other premiums - Could be a multitude of reasons (e.g., a tax on issuing certain loans).

The Finances of the Federal Reserve

The Fed's assets consist mainly of government bonds and mortgage-backed securities. The Fed's liabilities consist of currency outstanding and bank reserves.

The Fed receives interest on the government bonds and mortgage-backed securities it buys. However, the Fed does not pay interest on money held by the public. Therefore, the Fed's profits are large.

Even though the Fed is not a business, it does produce financial statements. The Fed typically follows Generally Accepted Accounting Principles (GAAP). These are created by an independent group of accounting experts. Most private businesses follow these rules as well.

However, the Fed does create some of its own accounting rules. The main difference in the Fed's accounting rules is the way it accounts for the bonds it owns. Most companies must value their bonds at the current market value. They then account for an unrealized gain or unrealized loss on their investments. However, the Fed accounts for its bonds at the price it paid for them. Most of the Fed's assets are government bonds or government-backed bonds.

Most of the Fed's liabilities are reserves, i.e., the amount owed to the member banks. Other liabilities include currency outstanding. These two liabilities are examples of money that the Fed creates out of thin air. In 2015, the Fed's assets exceeded its liabilities. This is called equity. Equity is primarily made up of the initial capital of banks.

An analysis of the financial statements shows that the Fed is not very solvent. The Fed does not have much of an equity cushion. The Fed's assets as of December 31, 2014, were $4,487 billion and capital was $56 billion. The capital ratio (capital divided by assets) was only 1.2 percent. In comparison, a well-capitalized bank usually has a capital ratio of about 10 percent.

The Fed does have a footnote in its financial statements disclosing its unrealized gains or losses. At the end of 2013, the Fed had unrealized losses on its bond portfolio of $53 billion. This would have essentially wiped out the equity of the Fed. However, at the end of 2014, the Fed had total unrealized gains of $174 billion.[36]

The market value of the bonds that the Fed holds is highly dependent on market interest rates. If market interest rates go down, the value of the bonds goes up. If interest rates go up, the value of the bonds go down. Because the Fed's monetary policy actions affect interest rates, its actions can have a huge impact on the value of the assets it holds.

Meanwhile, the Fed's liquidity and profitability are very strong. Liquidity is not an issue because the Fed can create additional cash at any time to pay off its bills.

The Fed is highly profitable because the interest it earns on the bonds it holds is a lot greater than the interest it pays on its reserves. The Fed doesn't pay any interest on the 1.37 trillion dollars currently in circulation.[37]

The Fed does incur a lot of operating expenses, which will be explained more in Part II - Fat Fed.

After accounting for expenses and paying the statutory dividend on the member banks' equity, the earnings are distributed to the U.S. Treasury, instead of flowing into equity (see chart 3). Therefore, equity and capital do not increase much over time.

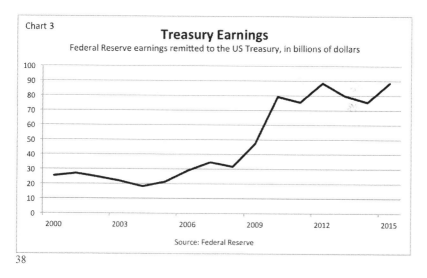

Chart 3
Treasury Earnings
Federal Reserve earnings remitted to the US Treasury, in billions of dollars

Source: Federal Reserve

38

The remittances to the Treasury are affected by how much the Fed spends on its operations. If it spends a lot, then remittances to the U.S. Treasury go down. In Part II - Fat Fed, I explain how the Fed spends a lot.

Part II: Fat Fed

Chapter 4: Competition Creates Efficiencies

*"Underlying most arguments against the free market
is a lack of belief in freedom itself."*
-Milton Friedman, Economist

Economic theory suggests that more competition in a marketplace creates more efficiency. This means that a society can create more goods and services using the same resources.

Efficiency

If you ask a businessperson why his or her company strives for efficiency, he or she will tell you the company must operate efficiently because it competes with other businesses that provide a similar product or service. If customers are dissatisfied with one company, they can go to another.

One way to compete is to offer a product at a lower price than competitors. If companies can reduce the cost of producing their product, or increase their output, they can offer their goods at a lower price.

Another way to compete is to offer a higher quality option than the competition. That's why some businesses invest in research and development; they want to improve their products and reduce their costs. Companies are driven to make their product cheaper and better so their products are chosen over competitors.

Companies in competitive environments can take drastic measures to increase efficiency. I know this from my experience working in private industry. I have seen firsthand what the power of money does to people in competitive environments.

The main goal of a company is to increase its owners' wealth by earning profits. Many companies directly reward employees for work that leads to increased revenues or decreased costs.

It is amazing to see what people do when a $20,000 bonus is on the line. A supervisor will fire a good employee in an effort to reduce costs. Managers spend time deciding how to cut costs in order to increase their own pay.

Some of this is distorted further by the principal-agent problem. In this case, the shareholders - the owners of the company are principals and the company's managers are agents. The shareholders want their companies to make as much money as possible. They hire managers to run their businesses. However, the managers have their own incentives to make as much money for themselves and do as little work as possible.

To resolve this problem, owners try to align the incentives of the managers as closely as possible to those of the owners. They use profit sharing, *stock* options, and other motivators to keep the managers on track. Larger businesses with more employees become even more difficult to manage. If one person owns and manages a small business, it is easy for the owner to oversee management. The owner of a few shares in a large corporation has very little influence in the selection of managers and executives.

I used to work in the investment department of a private-sector bank. When the bank acquired another bank, management decided that the bank did not need two investment departments, and got rid of the one from the newly acquired bank. This affected many people's lives because they lost their jobs. But this is how the private sector operates; it is efficient, competitive, and sometimes cutthroat.

Government Efficiency

The private sector is usually pretty efficient, but the government sector is less so. I learned this as an intern for the U.S. Government Accountability Office. This is Congress' watchdog organization, which reviews the efficiency and effectiveness of various government organizations. During my internship, I saw the inefficiency of government programs firsthand.

Government agencies usually face lower competitive pressures than do businesses. However, governments can face competition from other regional governments. If a city does not provide effective government services, or taxes are too high, people will vote with their feet and move to a different city. When this occurs, the prices of properties in the undesirable city usually fall and the prices of properties in the more desirable city increase. The difference in home prices between a desirable city and an undesirable city can reveal the cost of a poorly run government entity.

State governments are less susceptible to competition than are local governments because it is more difficult to move to another state than to another city. Someone dissatisfied with state government is less likely to move, because the geographic boundary is larger. National boundaries are larger yet, so national governments are more or less unaffected by competition due to their large geographic areas.

Despite a lack of competition, government entities still have an incentive to provide services somewhat efficiently.

Most government operations are funded with tax revenue. If too many people move away from a city with poor services or high taxes, the city may go bankrupt because not enough people are living there and paying taxes. Even if residents don't pick up and move somewhere else, they may complain to elected officials about high taxes. Officials want to get re-elected, so they do their best to keep their constituents happy.

Federal Reserve Efficiency

The Fed is an independent government organization that has some aspects of the private sector. I joined the Federal Reserve Bank of Minneapolis in 1996. The Fed appealed to me because it is not subject to the same risk that is associated with a private company; the Fed will never get bought out or go away unless Congress ends it.

I began working with automated clearinghouse transactions. ACH transactions are transfers of money to and from banks - like direct deposit of paychecks. The Fed processes these transactions, but charges a fee to do so. It felt like a regular business; we provided services to customers, and the customers paid us fees. We had to make more in fees than the costs we encountered. I was happy because I specialized in efficiencies, and I added value by reducing the costs of computer usage. The department's operations were very lean, and people were sometimes let go to reduce costs.

The priced services department of the Fed has not always been efficient. Before 1980, the Fed could compete unfairly by subsidizing these areas without regard to recouping costs. The Monetary Control Act of 1980 changed this. The act stipulated that several of the Fed's services must be priced services that compete with private sector operators. The Fed's services must recoup costs including the cost of capital (i.e., earn a profit). Private sector operators are able to compete on equal footing in these services.

Now, the Fed's priced services have private sector competition and are therefore more efficient than the noncompetitive portions of the Fed. The Fed charges banks a fee to deal with cash payments, facilitate electronic transactions, and process checks. The Fed charges fees for these services because it needs to recoup its costs in these services and earn a return on capital investment. If it charges too high a fee or have poor customer service, the customers could use private sector competitors.[39]

Priced Services

In the early 2000s, Congress passed the Check 21 Act, which allowed for an electronic image of a check to be a legal document. This permitted a very efficient payment option. An electronic transaction costs less than a penny to process, but a paper check costs more than a dollar to process. Before the act, about a quarter of the Fed's workforce was employed processing checks. This was part of the priced services area and required that the Fed recoup its costs and make a profit so it could compete against private-sector operators.

The Check 21 Act created a shift in the marketplace, and a great reduction in the demand for check processing services, as checks could now be processed electronically through image capture. As a priced service in a competitive environment, the Fed acted by closing numerous check processing centers, cutting down in size from 45 in 2003 to just one by 2010.[40]

One example of the cost-consciousness of priced services can be seen in its telephone support call answer rate. Departments, which must recoup their costs, answer a lower percent of phone calls. That is, they spend less to employ phone support staff. If you do not have to worry about recouping your costs, you can over-staff your call centers to answer all phone calls at peak times and let staff sit around during less busy times.

It is interesting to see the difference in cultures between the priced services department and other areas of the Fed. The other services provided by the Fed, like monetary policy, and bank regulation and supervision, have no competitors, and they do not have to earn money. As a result, there are fewer incentives to cut unnecessary expenses.[41]

Most of the Fed has little motivation to be efficient. The threat of unhappy constituents does not impact the Fed as directly as it would another government agency. There is very little *scarcity* because the Fed prints its own money and faces minimal budget constraints from Congress.

In the absence of scarcity, competition, and any incentive to be efficient, the Fed naturally has a tendency to become very fat. When I say "fat," I mean the Fed spends excessive amounts of money on unnecessary tasks, is inefficient, and lacks competitive motivation. The Fed creates money out of thin air, and is free to allocate it however it pleases. Chart 4 gives us a look at the priced services budget compared to the overall Fed budget.

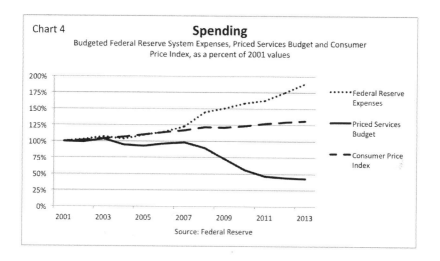

Chart 4 — **Spending**
Budgeted Federal Reserve System Expenses, Priced Services Budget and Consumer Price Index, as a percent of 2001 values
Source: Federal Reserve

Priced services expenses have gone down. Part of the reason is the huge reduction in check processing services as a result of market changes. Meanwhile, overall operating expenses have been growing faster than inflation. Part of the reason for this is the expansion of the Fed's responsibilities mandated by the Dodd Frank Act. (See chart 4)

It's not just the Fed; all central banks lack competitive pressures and are therefore prone to inefficiency. Part of central bank expenses are spent on research. Art Rolnick said the Fed's spending is comparable to or even more frugal than other countries' central banks. Foreign central banks are the best thing against which to compare the Fed because their objectives and expenses are the most similar, according to Rolnick.

The amount and cost of research varies by central bank. Miguel Sarmiento from Banco de la República—the central bank of Colombia—performed a study of 30 central banks around the world from 2000 to 2007. The study, which appeared in Banco de la República publication *Borradores de Economía*, compares research conducted by central banks through four indexes: output, demand, *productivity*, and relevance. Through those indexes, the research of the European Central Bank, the U.S. Federal Reserve Board of Governors, and the Bank of Canada performed the best. However, in Sarmiento's analysis of productivity and relevance of these banks, the Federal Reserve district banks had varying scores. Of the banks analyzed, the St. Louis Fed, was the best scoring district bank in productivity and relevance, coming in at number 8, while the Dallas Fed was the worst scoring district bank at number 29, between Ireland and Austria.[42]

Congressional Oversight

Fed management decides how much to spend on research as well as other operating expenses. The U.S. Congress has little effect on the Fed's budget. Usually, Congress is responsible for allocating funds to various government functions. Because Congress does not fund the Fed, the Fed can pretty much spend money on whatever it wishes.

I like to think of Congress as the parents who stay upstairs, and the Fed as Congress' teenagers downstairs; they can do whatever they please, so long as they don't burn the house down or wake up the parents.

The U.S. Congress does have some influence. It created the Fed, so it can destroy the Fed if its management truly misbehaves. The Fed's budget is not directly determined by Congress, but the Fed must operate within the expectations of Congress. As long as the Fed does not make Congress upset, it can spend as it pleases.

Art Rolnick said he thinks that taxpayers don't understand that the Fed's expenses ultimately cost them money, because money the Fed spends doesn't get remitted to the Treasury. Rolnick said if this was more widely understood, people might more heavily scrutinize the Fed's budget.[43]

Really extravagant spending like high management pay, naming rights on stadiums, or private jets, might get Congress' attention. The Fed does not pay exorbitant salaries to its top executives like some major corporations do. It does not buy the luxury boxes at professional football games. It does not provide funding to charities or political groups. This type of spending would wake up the sleeping parents.

Spending on some things like conferences, pensions, research, employee perks, outreach, and buildings doesn't usually upset congress. The Fed is careful to stay on Congress' good side. According to Nobel prize-winning economist Ed Prescott, the Fed could lose its independence by making Congress upset.

Even if the Fed did upset Congress, it would need a lot of momentum to create a bill and have the President sign it into law to punish the Fed. Congress knows the importance of the central bank and is leery of changing a system that has worked better than most other central banks around the world.

Fed Employee Motivations

Employees inside the Fed make decisions on what to spend money and how much to spend. These decisions are made without being constrained by scarcity or competition. Without these constraints, people turn to their personal motivations.

Fed employees have both intrinsic and extrinsic motivations. The intrinsic motivation is to do a good job and feel good about performing well. Therefore, they try to accomplish the three main responsibilities of the Fed (payment systems, supervision and regulation of banks, and monetary policy). They also have intrinsic motivation to do well for society, their friends, and families. People like power and prestige. People within the organization at the Fed also have extrinsic motivations. They like to get paid more, work in very nice environments, and travel to nice places.

Employees act on these motivations by spending the Fed's money - which ultimately comes from taxpayers. As a result of satisfying these goals, employees are generally happy.

People love to work at the Fed. I noticed that once people join the Fed, it's very hard for them to return to work in the private sector. I was amazed at the tenure of my coworkers. You were considered a new employee if you had only been working there for ten years. When I worked in the private sector, most employees would only stay for a couple of years.

Some would stay for five to ten years. Very few would stay for a career.

The next chapter and Appendix B provide detailed examples of spending money on activities that do not relate to the Fed's core mission.

I experienced this directly as I moved jobs within the Fed from an efficient priced services function to an inefficient non-priced services function.

Chapter 5: Club Fed

"Easy street
Easy street
Where the rich folks play
Yeah, yeah, yeah
Move them feet
Move them ever-lovin' feet"
From "Easy Street" in the play Annie

Part II – Fat Fed

After working for five years in the Fed's priced services Automated Clearing House division, I decided to get a job on the fat side. The fat side is like Club Med, the chain of all-inclusive resorts, where all of your wants and needs are cheerfully catered to.

From Lean to Fat

My transition to the fat side began in the Fed's well-appointed fitness center. While riding the stationary bike, I met an economist who worked in the non-priced services. I liked to read *The Wall Street Journal* while I rode and he liked to read *The Economist* magazine.

After several months, we became friends and an economist position opened up under him in the public affairs department. I applied for the position and submitted a sample article about the future of ecommerce. I still had to convince his department head that I was right for the position.

The department head invited me for an interview. I sat across the table from him in his big, ornate office. A large painting of the ancient Indian God Ganesh, who has the head of an elephant, hung on the wall. I took a year-long course on ancient Indian literature in college, so I asked him about the picture.

He told me he had interviewed many people at that table who were just as well dressed as me, and just as smart as me, but no one had ever asked about that painting.

I got the job.

Chapter 5 – Club Fed

When people ask how I became an economist, I tell them it was thanks to Ganesh (and a liberal arts education).

This transition from an analyst in the lean, mean priced services, to the genteel world of Public Affairs was remarkable. Gone was the huge stress that came with private sector competition. Instead, I was in an environment of deep thought.

I was responsible for taking the pulse of the regional economy. I enjoyed meeting with business leaders and finding out how their businesses were faring. Eight times a year I helped to write the "Summary of Commentary on Current Economic Conditions," more commonly known as the "Beige Book." This report helped the FOMC in making monetary policy decisions by providing information about the regional economy before any official data was released. I also helped with the Fed's economic education program, wrote articles for bank publications, and spoke at various association meetings. This was very intellectually stimulating.

It is interesting to work for an organization where some areas are very competitive and efficient while other areas are grossly inefficient. For example, people who work in priced services eat rather quickly, while others dine slowly on their subsidized food, leisurely looking out of huge windows of the cafeteria to the beautiful river. I would encourage anyone who gets invited to dine at the Fed to accept the invitation.

Part II – Fat Fed

Perks on the Fat Side

If an employee feels tired after a long lunch, he or she can go to a quiet room to sleep or meditate. Employees can walk the art-filled hallways, where it seems someone is always polishing the marble floors. They can stroll through the well-manicured grounds and stop to smell the flowers.

There are numerous perks associated with working at the Fed. These perks include both defined benefit and defined contribution pension plans, a Rolls-Royce-style health care plan, paid vacations, paid school tuition, a fitness center, subsidized meals, nice business travel, beautiful buildings and offices, a relaxed work atmosphere, and the ability to create projects in your own area of interest.

Pension benefits were so nice that I could retire at age 52 after only working at the Fed for 20 years. The defined contribution plan has a 100 percent matching contribution up to a certain percent of salary contributed by the employee. The investment options in the defined contribution plan are well-managed with very low fees.

In addition to the defined contribution plan, Fed employees also get a defined benefit plan that is based on years of service as well as the employee's age.

Retirees can also qualify for the excellent retirement healthcare plans. As I visited my main physician, my optometrist, my dentist, my dermatologist, my physical therapist, my chiropractor, and any other medical professionals, they all said to me, "Wow, you have great insurance!"

Chapter 5 – Club Fed

Besides my health insurance, the fitness center also kept me in shape. If I wasn't feeling very productive, I could go to the fitness center, which is open 24/7, and get my blood pumping. The center has a locker room, a weight room, machine area, and of course, a room for aerobics and yoga classes. When the weather was nice, I could also jog along the river.

In addition to caring for its employees' physical well-being, the Fed covers college tuition for employees to provide for their mental well-being.

The Federal Reserve Bank of Minneapolis has a strong partnership with the University of Minnesota. Several of the professors in the economics department at the University are also employees of the Fed. In addition, numerous grad students are paid research assistants of the Fed. It was very nice to take Ph.D. courses from professors who also worked at the Fed. It was also nice having study groups with students who were fellow Fed employees.

The beautiful views, the nice artwork, the gourmet subsidized lunches, paid classes, and the fitness center are all very nice, but this can grow old, so the employees like to travel. Because the Fed is a decentralized central bank with 12 district offices, numerous branches and the board of governors in Washington D.C., the need to travel and meet with each other to find out what's going on is ever-present.

For example, each district has economic education specialists. I am not sure why a central bank needs to teach economics - but hey, with the unlimited funds, why not? So, these economic education specialists get together every year at various locations like the Fontainebleau hotel in Miami Beach.

Part II – Fat Fed

What better place to discuss financial literacy than a river boat casino in Biloxi, Mississippi?

According to economist Dave Dahl, who started at the Minneapolis Fed in 1966, members of "Club Fed" used to fly first class, but this privilege was eventually seen as too ostentatious and revoked. The Fed must be careful not to wake its sleeping parents.[44]

Every year, prominent Fed economists attend a big event put on by the Kansas City Fed in the Grand Tetons. Fed officials discuss important papers and research on monetary policy at these meetings. Bank presidents and their research directors often attended the events. In Minneapolis, the Director of Research was Art Rolnick. I worked for Art and he is the finest human I have ever met.

Art is intelligent and compassionate. Art knows his limitations and asks advice from people in all levels of the organization from janitors to the president. Everyone working under Art was motivated to do well, and learned a lot from him.

Art is a master of public policy due to his crisp and clear thinking. An example of Art's clear thinking and strong *decision making* ability is his approach to evaluate a proposed public policy. This approach is one of the most valuable lessons I learned from Art.

The approach has three steps:

1) Why is the policy being proposed? Policies are usually proposed to solve a *market failure*. Market failures can fall into the following categories:

    a) *Externality* - costs or benefits outside of a market transaction

    b) Monopoly or *monopsony* - single seller or buyer

    c) *Public good* - *non-rivalrous* in consumption and *non-excludable*

2) Does the benefit of the proposed solution outweigh the costs?

If yes, the plan can proceed to step three.

3) Is there another solution that provides a larger net benefit?

If no, the proposed public policy has some merit.

Art's advice on policy analysis is one of the reasons I decided to write to write this book.

Dr. Rolnick has produced important research that relates to the Fed's mission. He is a money historian. He helped write "Market Discipline as a Regulator of Bank Risk," "In Order to Form a More Perfect Monetary Union," and "Looking for Evidence of Noncompetitive Behavior in Minnesota's Banking Industry."[45]

Part II – Fat Fed

Non-Fed Research

The Fed does a great deal of research that has little or no connection to the mission of the Fed, pouring large amounts of resources into these projects. Though some research conducted by Fed economists has little connection to the Fed's mission, it does have some benefits.

For example, Art Rolnick was widely quoted on the economic war among the states, where he criticized public financing by governments to lure businesses and build stadiums.

Another example is the work done by Art Rolnick and Rob Grunewald on early childhood development. This research showed huge long-term public returns to targeted scholarships for young children who are at risk of failing.

This research is very important and beneficial to society. The researchers traveled around the world promoting their findings. As a result, numerous cities, states, and countries are investing more into early childhood development. The world should see the benefits of this investment over the next few decades.

Even with this huge benefit to society, is it okay for the Fed to invest in research that is not clearly tied to the Fed's core mission? According to Art Rolnick, most of the Fed's research is tied to its mission.

In 1977, Congress passed the Community Reinvestment Act[46] (CRA). The act required banks to be held accountable to meet the financial needs of their communities. The act encourages banks to invest in local communities,

67

particularly in low-income and economically struggling areas. The Fed helps to ensure that banks are meeting these needs through their community outreach programs.

Rolnick said the Fed's research on Early Childhood Development is intended to help banks to achieve the CRA goals. The Fed's research helps banks to decide which investments provide the greatest benefits to society. In Art's opinion, early childhood education provides the best return on investment.

The community could benefit from research in a lot of areas. With a nearly unlimited supply of money, the Fed could theoretically invest in research on anything. My dad died of Alzheimer's. Should the Fed hire 100 researchers to study this disease? Maybe the Fed should increase the understanding of the structural supports of bridges, especially in light of the interstate highway bridge collapse in Minneapolis. If research in these categories helped banks better to invest in communities, the research would be a part of the Fed's mission.

Many of the economists, research assistants, and professors across the Federal Reserve System have the freedom to research topics that they are interested in that do not necessarily fit with money, banking, or the Fed.

Another example of unrelated research is the paper titled, "Do Minimum Wages Really Increase Youth Drinking and Drunk Driving?" written by M. Melinda Pitts in collaboration with economists Joseph J. Sabia and Laura Argys. This research references a study that found a positive correlation between minimum *wage* increases and youth (age 16-20) drunk driving fatalities. What was the purpose of this research, and how exactly would the findings benefit the Fed? Well, as it turns out, the only purpose of the research was to refute the aforementioned study. In the author's words, "We find little evidence that an increase in the minimum wage leads to increases in alcohol consumption or drunk driving among teenagers."[47]

I don't deny that this research is important, but in my opinion, the Fed should not fund this research.

Unnecessary Publications

The Fed also creates publications distributed for free. These publications contain stories from great economists with a wide range of interesting and helpful topics. Lots of stories in these publications have little relation to money, banking, or the Fed.

An example of this comes from the publication "Crossroads—Economic Trends of the Desert Southwest," published by the El Paso branch of the Dallas Fed. In the 2014 issue of "Crossroads," Dallas Fed economist Roberto Coronado writes, in partnership with Marycruz de Leon, an article titled, "Tourism and Recreation a Bright Spot in the Big Bend Region." Again, this is probably a helpful publication, especially if you live near El Paso. Does this help the Fed's mission more than research conducted on almost any other important topic, such as cancer?

Appendix B provides examples of Fed spending I believe to be unrelated to the Fed's mission.

Opinions vary widely on the costs and benefits of Fed research and publications. Nobel Prize-winning economist Ed

Prescott said the Fed has a lot of staff, but that they are all necessary. "It seems like we've got a lot of extra people, but we need that to politically maintain the system,"[48] he said. Rolnick argues that it's difficult to gauge the efficiency of a public good, like what the Fed produces, because there's no way to measure the output of the Fed. With no measurement of output, it's impossible to determine how efficiently the Fed operates. Rolnick said the Fed usually accomplishes its goals of stable prices and maximum employment - except during the 2008 financial crisis.[49]

Not only does the Fed invest in research that has little to do with its mission, but it also invests in many other seemingly irrelevant areas. The Fed creates numerous publications, provides support to community groups, provides economic and financial education, and supports a host of other unrelated initiatives, like the Minneapolis Fed's Center for Indian Country Development, whose mission is to help Native American communities across the nation reach their economic development goals.

The vagueness of the Fed's stated purpose allows the Fed to branch out into a variety of new issues. Some of these potential issues include intergenerational mobility in the economy, workforce development, and education in Indian Country. The president of the Minneapolis Fed, Narayana Kocherlakota, says he expects the Center for Indian Country Development to be "an important part of my legacy."[50]

The people in the organization can pursue their own wants and needs. Some people want more power, to achieve this they need more staff, and because there are no market constraints, they can get promotions and power by hiring more people.

Based on what I have seen at the Fed over the past 20 years, and my previous experience on corporate efficiencies, I believe the Fed could reduce spending on its own operations by 60 percent and still meet its core objectives.

Chapter 6: Bring in the Budget Slashers

"Frugality includes all the other virtues."
-Cicero, Philosopher

Part II – Fat Fed

The Fed performs numerous important functions. Some people think a few billion dollars a year in waste is nothing compared to the tremendous benefits a central bank offers.

There is an opportunity to cut the waste without hurting the core responsibilities of the Fed. However, if not done correctly, society could be worse off.

It could spell disaster if Congress tried to take control of the Fed's budget. First, Congress has incentive to use monetary policy to try to create short-term benefits of lower interest rates at the cost of long-term inflation. It is hugely important for a central bank to be independent, as evidenced by disasters across many countries whose politicians interfered with central bank operations.

Second, outside cuts forced onto organizations can create perverse incentives as the decision makers try to cause harm so the budgets can be increased again. This can be especially true for government organizations that do not have to worry about survival.

For example, when taxpayers get upset about government waste, they often make their views known. If politicians cut budgets, bureaucrats must respond. Sometimes the response is to stop providing the most important services. If you cut a vital function, people may respond by complaining to politicians to restore the function by providing more funding.

If you manage a government function, you like the fat. With reduced funding, you have to cut something. The taxpayers want you to cut the fat. The taxpayers still want the important public functions performed. The bureaucrat will sometimes think by cutting the muscle, taxpayers will lobby to increase the funding.

"Every year we go through something, but we're able to rally and say this is important, and then the funding comes,"[51] said Grace Araya, Director of Eyes on the Future Child Development Center in Rogers Park, IL, while discussing upcoming budget cuts to childcare in Illinois

It would be easier to cut the funding as productivity gains occur or expenditures unexpectedly decline. Like me, you probably know public sector employees who talk about having to buy something near the year-end. They say that they have money left in the budget and have to use it or lose it. In addition, they fear that if they come under-budget this year, then next year's budget will be reduced.

During the 2008 Financial Crisis, cuts were enacted in at least 46 states plus the District of Columbia. Cuts occurred in all major areas, including healthcare (31 states), services to the elderly and disabled (29 states and D.C.), K-12 education (34 states and D.C.), and higher education (43 states).[52] These programs were cut because taxes declined, not because need declined. In fact, during this time, the need increased as more families faced economic difficulties.

When cuts are all made at the same time during a recession, it can make the downturn even worse, as the 2008 Financial Crisis cuts required employee layoffs, cancelled contracts with vendors, and other decreases in economic activity

Part II – Fat Fed

The Fed Cuts

The Minneapolis Fed had high expenses due to its rural nature, which included many small banks, low population, and large geography.

Dahl recalled that Mark Willis became president and started to cut costs. Willis made changes to the Minneapolis Fed's budget to keep up with changing circumstances. One change was moving from a unit banking system with a lot of small banks and many correspondent banks to a national banking system. This raised questions regarding the necessity of district banks.

When asked if the Federal Reserve system still needs 12 district banks, Dave Dahl answered, "That's kind of a loaded question," and laughed. "The economy has changed," he said, "if you went back to 1913, you'd find roughly 30,000 banks. Today we are probably down to about 6-7 thousand. With interstate banking, we have banks that are operating on almost a national basis. That was not how the Fed was conceived. The Fed would serve banks in its region."

When asked about some of the costs of reducing the number of district banks, Dahl compared the situation to the allowance of interstate banks. When laws were passed to allow interstate banking, many banks began to merge. Each original bank needed to direct resources to have a board of directors, and maintain an independent status. By merging into one bank, they eliminated a lot of overhead costs. The same case could be made for the Fed, Dahl said. Making the district banks like branches and eliminating directors would reduce costs, but could have many other consequences as well.[53] The Fed was created as a decentralized central bank and reducing regional Fed responsibilities could change the power balance.

Discussions about the structure of the Fed have been ongoing since the Fed was established. Some proposed more Districts, while others proposed as few as five districts. President of the Kansas City Fed, Thomas Hoenig, said the 12 districts help to ensure decentralization of power, and geographic distribution of influence.

Hoenig said the district system has been an overall success. In response to questions about whether the Fed should have fewer districts, he said the number of districts is not logistically necessary, but does keep the power of the Fed in check. Hoenig also said the 12 districts weren't entirely necessary when the Fed was chartered either. "Even then, decades before today's high-speed technology, there was no compelling physical reason for having 12 Reserve Banks."

Hoenig said centralized national banks such as the first and second central banks may have operated more efficiently, but were much more prone to corruption, as in the case of bank president Biddle.[54]

These cuts could be made inside the Fed by using the private sector model. When companies become fat, they sometimes bring in a turnaround expert to cut expenses.

Companies' Cost Cutting Efforts

Sometimes for-profit companies also need to cut fat. The company's entrenched management (from the principal/agent problem) could continue to operate for a period of time, making strategic decisions that are terrible from the owner's perspective. After the company's financial performance deteriorates for a period of time, the board of directors is forced to take action. The board may fire the management and bring in a turnaround expert or a "hatchet man," someone whose purpose is to deeply cut costs, shut down departments, and lay off people.

IBM

In the 1990s, IBM, one of the country's largest companies, laid off more than 100,000 people[55]. In the 1980s, IBM's profit margins declined as costs remained level and profits declined. This was because IBM began to lag behind its competitors technologically, with Intel and Microsoft taking the lead.

MIT Sloan Management Review attributes IBM's downturn to customers' declining interest in mainframe computers.[56] In other words, one of their most profitable products was not selling well. Unfortunately, IBM executives did not see this coming and were unable to adjust and adapt in time. IBM failed to see the technological advances of the microcomputer that would soon to take over the market. IBM also began to allow its quality to slip. Customer service was at a low, quality of products was declining, and employees were led to believe that job security was unrelated to performance.

Essentially, IBM became too comfortable in its position as top dog. For a long time, it held a near monopoly on the PC. It believed it did not need to work as smart or hard in order to succeed. This sort of relaxed disposition often leads to financial problems for corporations, and they become fat.

In 1985 John Akers became the CEO of IBM after working for the company since the 1960s. When he became CEO, Aker ordered reorganization and a significant number of job cuts. Unfortunately, Akers' tenure as CEO saw IBM's first time operating at a loss as mainframe computer sales continued to tank. Despite his best efforts, Akers resigned.

Looking for a more dramatic shift in company orientation beyond layoffs and reorganization, the board hired Louis Gerstner Jr. as CEO. This brought about a change in the company's main objectives, steering it away from producing hardware and toward software and services. With these changes, IBM's stock went from $40 per share in 1993 to $175 per share in 1997.[57]

Canadian Pacific

Canadian Pacific Railway is an important transportation company that links eastern and western Canada. The railway has 14,000 miles of lines spanning across Canada and into the upper midwestern United States. Canadian Pacific Railway has had times of prosperity and times of financial trouble. Over time, Canadian Pacific Railway became fat and lost its competitive edge; costs of employment and other expenses began to rise.

Canadian Pacific Railway was able to sustain an inefficient environment for some time due to its huge market share and very few competitors. These inefficiencies hurt profits, making shareholders unhappy.

A new CEO, E. Hunter Harrison, was brought in as a turnaround expert to clean up the company. Harrison had been a railroad man his entire career, and saved Canadian Pacific Railway with his cost-cutting techniques. He was named Railroader of the Year in 2002 and 2015 by industry trade journal, *Railway Age*. Harrison is known for his tough and hard demeanor, a man who means business. According to Brian Stevens, the National Rail Director of the Canadian labor union, Unifor, "From a labour relations perspective, in terms of changing the culture, he has gone further, harder, more aggressive in issuing disciplines and terminating employees."

Under the directive of Harrison, a net 4,800 jobs from 19,500 employees have been cut. Harrison is taking other steps to eliminate costs and increase annual revenue growth. He repurposed previously abandoned space owned by the company into new offices, got rid of 400 older locomotives and 11,000 cars, shed some rail terminals, and initiated tougher disciplinary actions.

Harrison realizes this has created a tough environment; but, as he put it, "[Canadian Pacific Railway] was a horrible culture and they were heavy in fat." He also states that he may have created a culture of fear, but creating this culture may not have been such a bad thing. It was a mess he had to clean up; "Here's your job to do, do it, and if you don't, you are not going to get to stay. That looks to me a pretty simple contract. You can call it fear or accountability, responsibility, whatever, but it is just basic. The hard part is that someone created a culture of permissiveness, which means somebody else has to come in and make a change."

Employees and customers have complained that Harrison's changes created an exhausting and scary work environment, and led to poor customer service. But this may be the cost of running an efficient, competitive, and profitable company. Now that Harrison has whipped the company into shape, Keith Creel will become the new CEO of Canadian Pacific Railway in 2016. While Creel is just as much a railway man as Harrison, he is known to be a bit less intense and perhaps more even-keeled.[58] [59]

Target

The first Target store was built in St. Paul, Minnesota, in 1962 as a venture of the Dayton Company, which had been operating department stores since 1902. Target was meant to sell trendy clothes and housewares at prices lower than department stores. Soon, sales at Target stores began to exceed those at Dayton's department stores.

By 2000, Target accounted for more than 75 percent of the Dayton Company's profits. The company rebranded the same year, changing its name to Target Corporation. In 2004, Target Corporation sold its remaining department stores, now exclusively operating Target stores.

Target's growth and popularity peaked in the early 2000s. Target's popularity declined during the economic downturn. Cost-cutting efforts led to lower budgets for designers, which brought consumers' perceived value of Target to all-time lows.

Target's reputation was further hampered by a data breach in the fall of 2013, during which the credit card information of nearly 70 million customers was stolen.

Part II – Fat Fed

In early 2014, Target's CEO resigned in the midst of the recovery from the previous year's data breach. In August, the company brought on Brian Cornell, a former Pepsico and Sam's Club executive. Cornell's aim has been to steer Target back onto a path of growth. One of his first big moves as CEO was to call off Target's expansion into Canada.

Target began planning an expansion to America's neighbor to the north in 2011. The opening of Target's first Canadian stores was riddled with problems, especially difficulties in developing a new foreign supply chain. In January 2015, Cornell made the decision to axe the company's Canadian division in a move that was projected to cost around $5.4 billion.

While the shutdown was very expensive, it was expected to save the company a lot of money in the long run. Target's own estimates suggested that the Canadian division wouldn't turn a profit for at least 10 years. About 550 jobs were cut at the company's headquarters following the Canadian shutdown.

In March of 2015, Target announced to shareholders that it planned to eliminate "several thousand" corporate jobs in the next two years. In the months following this news, the company laid off 1,940 employees from its Minneapolis, MN, headquarters, eliminated another 1,400 open positions and laid off 180 employees at its technical support center in India.[60]

In June of 2015, Target announced the sale of its in-store pharmacies to CVS. Target said it expects the pharmacies to operate more efficiently and effectively under different management.[61] Earlier in 2015, Cornell also cut an unpopular streaming video service called Target Ticket.

Chapter 6 – Bring in the Budget Slashers

Cornell described his position as CEO of Target as a "dream job." He says his goal is to find what Target guests want, and deliver it to them.[62] He's spent lots of time talking to customers and employees to determine how better to operate the company. Essentially, Cornell is trying to cut Target's fat and strengthen its muscle.

Cornel was appointed as CEO of Target by shareholders who were concerned that the company was becoming unprofitable. This is a similar story to IBM and Canadian Pacific. When the companies were struggling to remain profitable, the new CEOs evaluated the company's businesses to cut unprofitable divisions, and expand in areas that showed potential growth.

Solution to Fat Fed

The solution to the "Fat Fed" problem is to bring in an outside turnaround expert as the Chair of the Federal Reserve System. Based on what I have seen at the Fed over the past 20 years and my previous experience with corporate efficiencies, I believe the Fed could reduce spending on its own operations by 60 percent and still meet its core objectives. An axe man could cut $3 billion dollars from annual spending; this is equivalent to giving every American household an additional $25 per year.

Part III: Friendly Fed

Chapter 7: Too Close to be Objective

"At the heart of the network are 147 financial institutions and central banks — especially the Federal Reserve, which was created by Congress but is owned by essentially a cartel of private banks."
-Karen Hudes, Lawyer

Friends with Benefits

The Fed is an organization with close relationships to banks.

In order to become a member of the Fed, banks are required to purchase stock in the Fed. For nationally chartered banks, membership is obligatory, but it is optional for state banks. Owning stock in the Fed is different from owning stock in a private company. The stock of the Fed cannot be traded or sold, does not have a claim on the assets or earnings of the Fed, and shareholders do not vote on all board members. It does earn a 6 percent dividend per year as defined by law, and allows the holder to recommend 6 of the 9 Fed board members.

Employees of the Fed want to be friendly with member banks, and employees of member banks want to be friendly with the Fed. The Federal Reserve System is designed in a way that promotes close relationships with private banks. Consider the Fed's board of directors.

Each district bank has a nine-member board of directors, made up of three types of directors: three class A directors, three class B and three class C. Fed member banks recommend the class A and B directors, and the Board of Governors appoints the Class C directors. As required by the Federal Reserve Act, Class A directors of each Reserve Bank represent the member banks within the Federal Reserve District. Class B and Class C directors represent the public and may not be officers, directors, or employees of any bank.

Furthermore, Class C directors may not be stockholders of any banks.[63] (see Chart 5)

Chart 5

	Class A	Class B	Class C
Serves	Member Banks	The Public	The Public
Appointed/ Elected By	Elected by Fed Member Banks	Elected by Fed Member Banks	Appointed by Board of Governors
Restrictions	None	May not be officers, directors, or employees of any bank	May not be officers, directors, or employees of any bank. May not be stockholders.

Source: Federal Reserve

Conflict of Interest

The close relationship between the Fed and member banks creates a conflict of interest, which is often scrutinized. In response to intense criticism following the financial crisis, the Fed made changes to its policy "to ensure that Reserve Bank boards reflect an appropriate cross-section of industry and the public."

The new policy more clearly establishes bank affiliations, which could cause a conflict of interest, and sets requirements in place for bank-affiliated directors to resolve conflicts of interest by resigning from the Fed, or ceasing affiliation with other financial institutions.[64]

Fed and Banks Work for Each Other

The Fed hires a lot of bankers to work on examinations. Banks hire a lot of Fed employees to work for them. The Fed tries to get around this inherent conflict of interest by temporarily preventing former Fed employees from accepting jobs at big banks.

The following list of former Fed officials illustrates the close ties between the big banks and government.

William Dudley: president of the Federal Reserve Bank of New York since 2009. Formerly served as chief economist and managing director of Goldman Sachs from 1986 to 2007.[65]

Timothy Geithner: Current president and managing director of private equity firm Warburg Pincus. Former president of the Federal Reserve Bank of New York from 2003 to 2009, and Secretary of the Treasury from 2009 to 2013.[66]

Edward Gerald Corrigan: partner and Managing Director at Goldman Sachs since 1996. Former President of the Federal Reserve Bank of Minneapolis, from 1980-1984, and New York from 1985-1993.[67]

Henry Paulson: secretary of the U.S. Treasury from 2006-2009. Worked for Goldman Sachs from 1974-2006.[68]

These are merely a few examples of government officials who previously worked for big banks.

Working for both a private bank and the Fed or Treasury can be dangerous because the employees may have a strong bias and are very influential. MIT economists Daron Acemoglu and Simon Johnson explain the way banks influence the Fed: "Bankers are persuasive; many are smart people, armed with fancy models, and they offer very nice income-earning opportunities to former central bankers."[69]

People Are Generally Good

The Fed's role as a watchdog has often been called into question when its policies benefit the interests of banks or large corporations more than those of the country as a whole. I don't think the people who make these decisions are intentionally colluding. I believe that most people try to do the right thing, but everyone is swayed by their biases.

I have spoken with many groups of people. Each group truly believes that it is a very important—if not the most important—contributor to society. Farmers believe they are the most important because without food, people would starve. Teachers believe they are the most important because they are educating the next generation of workers.

People work in professions and careers not only because they need money, but often because they want to improve society.

Most of the bankers and Fed employees are outstanding people. They care about their work and want it positively to impact society. They care for the financial well-being of local people and neighborhoods.

People do what they believe to be the "right thing" based upon their own perspective and biases. Because many of the Fed's employees have previously worked for private banks, a conflict of interest may easily arise.

Imagine you are an agent for the FBI and you learn that your mother is accused of treason and being sentenced to death. Would you spend more time assisting the system that arrested your mother, or discussing alternatives to the death sentence? It would be nice to find a way to rehabilitate her and help her to lead a crime-free life.

Most people would do the "right thing," and work toward a plan that did not involve the death of their mother. Similarly, someone who worked for an organization like a bank and has connections at the organization probably wants to see the bank succeed. When these individuals work for the Fed, they might support policies that favor banks.

Right Thing Gone Bad

Fed employees can unintentionally act upon their biases, just like everyone else.

If a great person and long-time bank worker joins the Fed as an examiner or a policy maker, he or she may hold a bias toward his or her previous employer. When a policy maker has to make a tough decision about how to handle a failing bank, he or she might not even contemplate shutting the bank down.

For example, say Susan is a great person, who spent a long time working for Bank X. She recently accepted a job as a regulator at the Fed. When Bank X goes through some hard times and becomes insolvent, the Fed has to make the tough decision about how to deal with the bank.

In Susan's mind, shutting the bank down is out of the question. Not only does Susan like the bank and the people who work there, but she is used to looking at things from a bank employee's point of view. She is likely to be more lenient and understanding with the executives of the bank. She tries to do the "right thing" by "saving" the bank.

As described in Chapter 3, the Fed was essentially created to ensure the stability of the American financial system. One of the Fed's four primary responsibilities according to its website is:

"Supervising and regulating banks and other important financial institutions to ensure the safety and soundness of the nation's banking and financial system and to protect the credit rights of consumers."[70]

Moral Hazard

The Fed's job is to shut down insolvent banks. If the Fed does not act to shut down banks, the banking system becomes less stable. As stated in Chapter 2, banks have an incentive to take on risk. Bailing out failed banks further encourages banks to take risk. Banks act as if they are invincible because they think that Fed regulators will ignore bad behavior, or the government will bail them out.

According to research by the Minneapolis Fed, bailing out banks is a source of *moral hazard*. When the Federal Government saves failing banks, it provides an incentive for these banks to continue to make risky investments in the future. The bankers then may think, "I can take on high-risk high-reward loans because the Federal Government will save my bank if I lose too much!"

As an alternative to bailouts, the Minneapolis Fed proposed three measures to reduce the risk of bank failures and contagion. The three proposals are:

Early Identification: The process of identifying and responding "to the material exposures among large financial institutions and between these institutions and capital markets." When a large financial institution performs an action that seems risky to Fed policymakers, those policymakers have a knee-jerk reaction to save the financial institution. Often, these risky actions don't severely hinder these institutions, so saving them is a waste of government resources. However, there are risky actions, which lead to failure more often than others. The purpose of early identification is to distinguish between the actions that require intervention and the actions that don't.

Enhanced Prompt Corrective Action: "Requiring supervisors to take specified actions against a bank as its capital falls below specified triggers." Essentially, enhanced prompt corrective action closes banks while they still have positive capital in order to reduce the effect on other financial institutions or capital markets.

Stability-Related Communication: Communication between policymakers and creditors to ensure that creditors are aware of the new efforts of policymakers (early identification and enhanced prompt corrective action). "Creditors will not know about efforts to limit spillovers, and therefore will not change their expectations of support, absent explicit communication by policymakers about these efforts."[71]

By monitoring the stability of firms, or even by closing them before they begin to incur damaging losses, the Fed would be able to ensure the stability of the system by closing firms before they incur losses that could bring down their peers. Nobel Prize-winning economist Ed Prescott believes that the Fed should stay out of bank bailouts in most cases. "A few banks going bankrupt is no big deal. Lots of industries have big bankruptcies," he said.[72]

Too Big To Fail

During the most recent financial crisis several huge financial companies became insolvent. Rather than shutting them down, the Fed and the Treasury decided to save them.

The rationale was that these institutions were so large and interconnected that if they were shut down, contagion would occur throughout the whole financial system. Meaning, if one bank goes down, and they owe money to another bank, the other bank will go down, and this domino effect could occur throughout the entire financial system. Many didn't consider the possibility that the government nationalize these banks, which would have kept the contagion to a minimum.

Part III – Friendly Fed

U.S. leaders gave the American people two options: bail out the banks, or let them slip into bankruptcy and create contagion.

The leaders, who are good people and care about their country, could not fathom that the company where they had worked for decades would disappear. Their resumes would have big holes in them. Their friends and colleagues would blame them for losing their livelihoods. Shareholders would be wiped out. Vulture funds would pick over the carcass of the company they built.

If someone worked for a bank and then began a job at the Fed, it raises the concern that he or she holds a bias in favor of the bank. On the other hand, when someone begins a job at a bank after working at a regulatory institution like the Fed, it raises the concern that he or she was doing favors for the bank in exchange for compensation later.

It is easy to blame these people; but, in the same situation, many with the same biases would have made the same decisions.

Another policymaker had a different perspective and biases. Former Secretary of the U.S. Treasury, Lawrence Summers, an official without a long history on Wall Street, suggested nationalizing some large banks during the crisis, according to a book by another former Secretary of the Treasury, Timothy Geithner.[73] His suggestions were not taken.

The former Fed Director of Research, Art Rolnick, said he wouldn't nationalize banks. Instead, he said he would require them to hold a lot more capital to secure their investments.[74] This is discussed more in Chapter 9.

I believe Summers was overruled because the bias for supporting Wall Street was too strong.

New York Fed Too Powerful?

Many criticize the Federal Reserve System, especially the Federal Reserve Bank of New York, for being too closely tied to big banks. The criticism became especially strong after bailouts of major financial institutions like AIG. Prescott essentially considers the New York Fed a part of the executive branch of the U.S. government, not an independent entity, free of political influence.

Some economists and lawmakers have raised questions about whether the New York Fed has too much power. Many of the nation's largest and most powerful banks are headquartered on Wall Street in New York City, which means they are regulated by the Federal Reserve Bank of New York.

A hearing was held to investigate the relationship between the Fed – particularly the New York Fed – and large banks. However, New York Fed President William Dudley protested the hearing, objecting to the premise that his term at the Fed was riddled with failures in judgment.[75]

Questions about the relationship between Wall Street and the New York Fed were especially prominent during the presidency of Timothy Geithner.

Art Rolnick believes Geithner had something to do with the financial crisis. "In 2008, in particular, we screwed up big time," he said. "I would blame Tim Geithner, who was the president of the New York Fed at the time. It was his job to make sure that all of those banks in New York were stable."[76]

The New York Fed has a permanent vote at the Federal Open Market Committee, but the other 11 district banks only vote once every three years on a rotating basis. The New York Fed also directly performs open market operations. This is a large responsibility, which some economists believe should not fall into the hands of only one district bank.[77]

The New York Fed has also been criticized for looking the other way while Citigroup kept $1.2 trillion in assets off of its balance sheet when Geithner ran the New York Fed and Jack Lew was at Citigroup.[78]

The New York Fed has close ties to the government. Edward Prescott asked, "What happened to the stock value of banks when Timothy Geithner [former head of the New York Fed] moved to [the] Treasury?" "They jumped in value," he answered, implying that Wall Street firms benefitted financially from Geithner's appointment.

Similarly, in a paper published by the University of California Berkeley, researchers found that stock prices reacted to news from FOMC meetings before information was released to the public. This implies that some traders had access to FOMC meeting information before it became available to the public.[79]

Prescott also questioned the influence of the government on the Fed. He believes the Fed has a close relationship with the president of the United States, "The Fed is and always has been in the pocket of the President ...Wall Street financed Obama's election."[80]

Stress Test

The government tried to stop the bailouts from happening again by passing a law that requires large banks to create "living wills" that describe how to shut down should they become insolvent.

In addition, the regulators were instructed to conduct analyses of these companies' businesses and conduct a "what if" analysis, also known as "stress tests."

The Federal Reserve Board, along with the FDIC and the Office of the Comptroller of Currency, were required to "stress-test" banks in accordance with the Dodd-Frank Act. Stress tests measure the amount of capital and risk that banks hold, in order to determine whether the banks stand on firm financial ground.

For the Dodd-Frank Act Stress Test, banks valued at over $10 billion must run tests under three different scenarios. These scenarios include a baseline scenario, an adverse scenario, and a severely adverse scenario. The adverse and severely adverse scenarios are not forecasts, but instead are designed to test the strength and resilience of the banks. Each scenario includes 28 variables, including economic activity, unemployment, exchange rates, prices, incomes, and interest rates. There are different scenarios for companies valued between ten and fifty billion dollars and for companies valued at over fifty billion dollars.[81]

In addition to the Dodd-Frank Act Stress Test, the Fed also uses the Comprehensive Capital Analysis and Review (CCAR)[82]. The CCAR test requires the bank holding company to submit annual capital plans to the Fed for review. The annual capital plan must have four specific elements. The first element is an assessment of the expected uses and sources of capital that reflect the bank holding company's size, complexity, risk profile, and scope of operations. Second, the Fed requires a detailed description of how the bank holding company assesses its capital adequacy. The third element it needs is the bank holding company's capital policy. For the fourth element, it asks for a discussion of any baseline changes to the holding company's business plans that are likely to have an impact on the bank holding company's capital adequacy or liquidity.

Still Too Big To Fail?

America's five largest banks – JPMorgan Chase, Bank of America, Citigroup, Wells Fargo, and US Bank – are disproportionately large in comparison with other U.S. banks. Together they hold nearly 7 trillion dollars in assets – about 45 percent of the entire American banking industry in 2014. These banks' share of the market grew more than two percentage points since 2013.[83]

Small banks have been falling out of favor for some time, especially following the financial crisis of 2008. The number of banks in the United States fell by more than half between 1990 and 2014. Meanwhile, the average size of banks has increased by about five fold.[84] [85]

The increase in size of banks has raised concerns from some economists that larger banks are more risk-prone. Larger banks typically have more complex organizational structures, higher debt to capital ratios, and are more involved in financial markets.[86] These factors were mentioned, among other things, in a study done by the International Monetary Fund (IMF) that evaluated the riskiness of big banks.[87]

Those skeptical of big banks also point out that smaller banks are less likely to take dramatic risks. Furthermore, in the case that a smaller bank fails, the bank's closure does not dramatically damage the American financial system. The bank would not be "too big to fail" and would not require a bailout.

On the other hand, others argue that larger banks benefit consumers by taking advantage of *economies of scale.* This means that large banks are able to operate more efficiently than smaller banks.[88]

Big or small, all banks have an incentive to take on risks. The regulators are assigned to make sure they follow the rules.

Chapter 8: Asleep at the Wheel

"I believe that the market is slowly waking up to the fact that the Federal Reserve is a clueless organization. They have no idea what they're doing. And so the confidence level of investors is diminishing, in my view."
-Marc Faber, Swiss Investor

In addition to taking it easy on the huge banks, regulators have failed to adequately supervise smaller banks. This lack of oversight created huge losses to the FDIC insurance fund. The following are some examples of bank failures.

One example was the failure of Chicago-based Corus Bank. First chartered as Aetna State Bank in Illinois in 1913, Corus Bank specialized in commercial lending. Beginning in 2003, it narrowed its focus from its historical concentration in commercial real estate to a subcategory: residential condominium construction, rehabilitation, and conversion loans.

In 1996, Corus had total assets of about $2 billion. Commercial real estate comprised 40 percent of its outstanding loans. By 2006, Corus' total assets had quintupled to nearly $10 billion, and commercial real estate loans made up 98 percent of its loan portfolio. By 2009, Corus had failed.

The 2012 Audit Report from the Office of Inspector General at the Department of the Treasury (OIG) describes the results of a review of Corus Bank's failure as well as the Office of the Comptroller of the Currency's (OCC) poor supervision of Corus.

Corus specified its investments in condo construction in regions with volatile housing markets. The report from the OIG concluded that Corus' failure was caused in part by its considerable investment in the waning commercial real estate markets and poor loan management procedures.

Part III – Friendly Fed

The market collapse that began in 2007 was particularly severe in many of Corus' principal market locations, and thus Corus' efforts to concentrate its assets in specific high-flying markets across the country ultimately proved to be catastrophic. Because lending in commercial real estate comprised 98 percent of Corus' investment portfolio, the reduction in value of real estate devalued many of Corus' assets.

Corus' poor investment strategy, lack of effective management, and poor loan administration contributed to its eventual downfall. As mentioned earlier, the OCC's poor supervision of Corus was one of the key factors in the bank's eventual downfall. Prior to 2008, OCC examiners praised Corus repeatedly for its high-quality management information systems and thorough credit files. However, following an examination in 2008, the OCC determined that:

1. Corus had not consistently performed timely and accurate appraisals to support the value of its loans.

2. Corus had inappropriately re-extended loans without reappraisals in situations where condominium sales were strong, but property prices were falling.

The bank logged record earnings in 2006 with a net income of $189 million. Corus' success in 2006 led to the OCC giving them a near-perfect CAMELS rating, grading it a 1 in all categories except the quality of its assets, which was graded as a 2. CAMELS, as you may recall, is the OCC's way of rating a bank's likelihood of failure and stands for **C**apital, **A**ssets, **M**anagement, **E**arnings, **L**iquidity, and **S**ensitivity.

You may also remember that, in Chapter 3, there was a second S, for systemic risk. This was not added until after the passage of the Dodd-Frank Act in 2010. However, the following examinations saw Corus' CAMELS rating steadily increasing until it reached the maximum of 5 in all categories by May 2009.

According to one OCC examiner, the fact that Corus had not experienced net losses for almost 20 years led management to believe that the bank would be invulnerable to the looming economic recession. Management believed that Corus' strong capital and liquidity positions would enable the bank to withstand any economic downturn.[89]

The Fed, after failing to recognize the apparent red flags of Corus' downfall, finally intervened during the twilight of Corus' existence. In February of 2009, the Fed signed a letter of agreement outlining requirements that Corus had to meet in order to remain open.

Included in this letter were clauses saying that Corus may not take dividends or any other form of payment, nor was it allowed to declare or pay dividends that resulted in a reduction in capital without prior written approval of the Reserve Bank and the Director of the Division of Banking Supervision and Regulation. In addition, the company was not allowed to buy or sell its own shares without the prior approval from the Fed. Corus also had to submit a plan to maintain sufficient capital.[90] In essence, the Fed wanted Corus to increase its capital ratio.

The Fed's letter did not prevent the owners or managers from selling their stock before the bank was shut down on September 11, 2009. Robert Glickman, beneficial owner of 20 percent of Corus common stock, disposed of 763,751 shares of common stock, or roughly 1.4 percent of all shares of Corus Bankshares, Inc.[91] Throughout June of 2009, Glickman continued to dispose of 15.6 percent of common stock at prices up to $0.46 per share.[92] These large disposals of common stock allowed Glickman and other owners to get money out before its downfall.

As of December 31, 2011, the FDIC estimated the bank's closing would cause a loss of $797.9 million to the Deposit Insurance Fund, which is funded by taxpayers, like you and me.[93]

Suspicious activity at Corus Bank should have raised some red flags to the supervisors at the OCC and the Fed. These red flags included:

- Rapid growth.
- Concentration of risk in their assets.
- Geographic concentration of their assets.
- Incentives to loan officers.

Rapid growth is a red flag because as banks take on more and more loans, the risk of each of those loans increases. As stated earlier, the value of Corus' assets nearly quintupled over 10 years. In the Corus Bankshares 2004 Annual Report, CEO Rob Glickman reports that the bank's commercial real estate portfolio grew from $3.8 billion to $5.3 billion over the year, a growth of $1.5 billion, nearly 40 percent.

Because Corus concentrated most of its new loans in the condominium construction market, it avoided one of the most basic principles of risk aversion: diversification of assets.

You may be familiar with the adage, "Don't put all of your eggs in one basket." Commercial real estate and construction loans made up 98 percent of Corus' portfolio in 2006. In other words, Corus put 98 percent of its eggs into the real estate basket. When this basket fell to the ground (i.e., the housing market crashed), all of its eggs shattered. Thus, it was a very risky move for Corus to concentrate its loans in such a manner. When banks make these types of moves, it is a huge red flag for future collapse. The regulators should have intervened, yet failed to do so, despite Corus' growing lack of diversification. According to the 2004 Annual Report, 76 percent of Corus' commercial real estate portfolio was comprised purely of condominium loans. In the report, CEO Robert Glickman said:

"Corus has pursued several unorthodox strategies in our commercial real estate lending business. First, investing such a large portion of a bank's assets in commercial real estate loans is unusual in the banking industry and could be considered a 'concentration of risk.' While we understand this approach brings with it certain risks, we feel that it is important to focus on the business that we know best. Corus has been originating increasingly larger commercial real estate loans and we believe we have developed considerable expertise in this market."

Glickman himself admits that investing so much in commercial real estate loans is "a concentration of risk" and "unusual in the banking industry." Yet, no one saw this red flag.

The geographic location of Corus' assets also should have been a red flag for Fed officials. Corus focused its investments in areas with volatile housing markets. Additionally, Corus had no offices in these areas to oversee its assets. The concentration of Corus' assets on condominium construction with narrow geographic range further contributed to the riskiness of Corus' portfolio.

The last red flag that the Fed should have noticed was the "unique compensation program" that Corus was offering loan officers who originated new business. The program paid an aggregate of $8.9 million to the top ten loan officers at Corus. The problem with offering a compensation program like this is that loan officers will then want to make more and more loans. The more loans they make, the more likely those loans will be risky. Riskier loans increase the likelihood that the Fed will have to intervene. Offering a program like this is a big red flag that a bank may be failing soon.[94]

Many other banks across the country were shut down during the 2009 financial crisis. The stories of these banks share many similarities with the story of Corus Bank's shutdown. The banks often had highly concentrated and risky investments, and were plagued by poor management. Several more examples of bank closures are listed below.

Other Bank Failures

Midwest Bank and Trust Co. was closed by the Illinois Department of Financial Professional Regulation on

May 14, 2010, after receiving enforcement actions from the Federal Reserve Bank of Chicago, and the Illinois Department of Financial Professional Regulation in December of 2009. The enforcement action taken against Midwest Bank had all parties agreeing: within 60 days, the board of directors of Midwest Bank would submit a written plan to strengthen board oversight of the management and operations of the bank. It were also required to submit a plan to strengthen its credit management. The bank was also required not to extend or renew any credit that the Report of Examination had deemed a "loss." It was also not allowed to extend or renew any credit to borrowers that had been classified "doubtful" or "substandard" without the prior approval of the bank's board of directors. The bank was later shut down because it failed to achieve all but one of the four goals in the plan it submitted, which included loan diversification, funding source diversification, capital fundraising, and double-digit loan growth. The FDIC estimated that the closure resulted in a loss of around $216 million to the Deposit Insurance Fund. Later, in 2013, the FDIC sued the former directors of the bank for gross negligence. As of July 2015, this lawsuit is still ongoing.[95]

Olde Cypress Community Bank was based in Clewiston, Florida, and had four other offices throughout Hendry and Polk Counties in Florida. The bank was opened in January of 1927. The Office of Thrift Supervision closed Olde Cypress on July 16, 2010. The bank had $169 million in assets as of March 31, 2010, and is estimated to have cost the Federal Deposit Insurance Corporation $31.5 million. The primary cause of the failure of Olde Cypress Community Bank was its aggressive growth strategy. It gave out family, nonresidential, and land loans. It also diversified its lending to other parts of Florida during the height of the real estate bubble. Unfortunately, this diversification resulted in Olde Cypress Bank lending to some of the areas in Florida that experienced the greatest depreciation rates during the economic crisis. These loan losses eventually led to the failure of Olde Cypress Community Bank.[96]

Turnberry Bank was opened in April of 1985 and had its main office in Aventura, Florida. In addition to its main office, it also had three branches, located in the Florida cities Pinecrest, Coral Gables, and South Miami. The Office of Thrift Supervision closed Turnberry on July 16, 2010. As of March 31, 2010, Turnberry had $263.9 million in total assets. The Federal Deposit Insurance Corporation estimates the loss to the Deposit Insurance fund at $34.4 million. There were three primary causes in the failure of Turnberry Bank. One was its aggressive growth strategy. The second was its "excessive concentrations in higher-risk loans." These included multifamily, nonresidential real estate, construction, land, and non-mortgage commercial loans. The third reason was that the bank did not have enough capital in relation to the risk level of its loans. These factors, in addition to the declining real estate market, resulted in substantial loan loss, which led to the failure of Turnberry Bank.[97]

Western Springs National Bank and Trust opened in January 1916. It had two offices: one was in Western Springs, Illinois, and the other in Countryside, Illinois. The Office of the Comptroller of the Currency closed Western Springs on April 8, 2011. The bank had $186.8 million in total assets as of

December 31, 2010. The loss to the Deposit Insurance Fund was estimated by the Federal Deposit Insurance Corporation to be $34 million dollars. Western Springs National Bank and Trust was in an unsafe or unsound condition to transact business. This caused substantial dissipation of assets or earnings. In addition, the bank incurred or was likely to incur losses that would lose all of its capital; there was no reasonable chance for recovery without federal assistance. These conditions were considered likely to seriously prejudice the interests of the DIF and the bank was severely undercapitalized. It was on these grounds that the OCC closed down Western Springs National Bank and Trust. The main causes of such dire straits for the bank were significant commercial real estate concentrations, bad credit administration, and poor risk management practices. Another factor in the bank's failure was the poor performance of loans purchased from Mutual Bank of Harvey, Illinois, a failed institution at which the Chairman of the Board for Western Springs was Vice Chairman.[98]

United Americas Bank, National Association was located in Atlanta, Georgia. It had branches throughout the Atlanta metropolitan area. The Office of the Comptroller of the Currency closed it on December 17, 2010. The FDIC estimated a loss to the Deposit Insurance Fund of $78.5 million. Some of the reasons for closure were that the bank experienced a substantial depletion of assets due to unsound practices, there was no reasonable way for the bank to regain solvency, and the bank was critically undercapitalized. The primary causes of the failure were large concentrations of risk in commercial real estate, inadequate risk management practices, weak oversight by the board of directors, and the lack of core funding sources. In addition, a number of loans that the bank made were mortgage loans to first-time homebuyers using individual tax identification numbers. These numbers are issued to foreign employees of U.S. corporations, and so when Georgia made stricter immigration laws, many of these individuals became unemployed and were unable to remit payment on their loans. Then, during the housing bubble pop in 2008, the loan portfolios significantly deteriorated. The board and management were slow to react and by 2010, the unsafe credit practices resulted in declining asset quality and increased losses that ate away at the capital.[99]

Carolina Federal Savings Bank was located in South Carolina. It had one main office and one branch in Charleston County, South Carolina. The OCC closed Carolina Federal Savings Bank on June 8, 2012. The bank had about $54.4 million in total assets, and the closure resulted in a loss of $17.1 million to the Deposit Insurance Fund. The OCC closed the bank because it had experienced a large dissipation of assets due to its unsafe practices, likelihood to incur losses that would deplete all of its capital, and failure to submit an acceptable capital restoration within the time allotted. Concentration in subprime single-family mortgage loans and commercial real estate loans, poor credit management practices, and an ineffective board of directors led to the bank's failure. The bank had been criticized numerous times by both the Office of Thrift Supervision and the Office of the Comptroller of Currency. Despite this, they failed to address weaknesses in concentration risk management, problem loan identification, underwriting of loans and problem loan modifications, allowance for loan and lease losses, and real estate-owned administration. Ineffective management weakened the bank, and a sharp downturn in the South Carolina real estate market dealt the bank's death blow.[100]

Regulators Have Failed

Sometimes banks can and do fail. Regulators can and do fail in their responsibilities to catch bad banks. All regulators, not just the Fed, are charged with reducing this possibility by examining bank practices for excessive risk. The next chapter provides some potential solutions.

Chapter 9: Become Less Friendly to Banks

"The problem is that while the Fed is largely independent of politicians, it is intimately connected, and even answerable, to the financial institutions that it is supposed to regulate."
-Stephen Haber and Ross Levine,
Wall Street Journal

Chapter 9 – Become Less Friendly to Banks

The previous chapters discussed how the Fed and other regulators are friendly to banks, causing huge bailouts and losses to the FDIC. Some people call this *regulatory capture.*

Regulatory capture describes the situation in which regulators, like the Fed, fall under the control of the organizations they are supposed to be regulating. When a regulator is "captured," it serves the interests of the industry it is supposed to regulate, instead of the public.

Retired Fed economist Art Rolnick said Timothy Geithner is a great example of a captured regulator. He referenced a book called *Too Big to Fail,* published by Minneapolis Fed economists, which highlighted problems with the regulatory system. Rolnick said the Fed was providing way too much insurance to banks. "If they got in trouble, we'd bail them out," he said.[101]

In the wake of the bailouts of banks and other financial institutions during the 2008 financial crisis, many lawmakers and citizens were concerned that regulators at the Fed held a bias toward major financial institutions. In the spring of 2015, lawmakers reviewed the Fed's procedures to determine the best plan to overcome the threat of regulatory capture. Currently, Fed regulators who oversee a financial institution are forbidden from taking employment at the institution for one year after leaving the Fed.[102] Some lawmakers are suggesting a tightening of this rule.

The Fed should reduce outside influence in the supervision and regulation of banks. To do this, the Fed should implement three solutions: require higher capital standards,

112

limit bank ownership and control of the Fed, and limit the Fed's disregard for regulations.

Require Higher Capital Standards

If bankers were required to have 100 percent equity, the banking system would become more stable. This would eliminate the "other people's money" problem. If banks put only their own money on the line, there would be less need for supervision and regulation. If banks had to worry about losing their own money, they would avoid risky investments without guidance from regulators

Nobel Laureate Ed Prescott recommends using a 100 percent equity banking system. Some financial firms would perform transaction services such as paying bills and cashing checks. Others would make loans to people using the bank owners' money.

Some of this has already occurred with peer-to-peer lending conducted by websites like Lending Tree and Prosper. Individuals who have money to lend are matched with people who want to borrow. Many people with savings can contribute a small amount of money to a particular borrower. One borrower may have hundreds of lenders each contributing $25.

If traditional banks are required to hold more capital, they tend to take less risk. This would result in fewer loans being made. Art Rolnick said he would like to see large banks have more capital or "skin in the game."[103]

Stop Private Banks from Owning and Influencing the Fed

Currently member banks are required to own stock in the Fed. As a result, they get a statutory 6 percent dividend.[104] In addition, they get to nominate six of the nine members of the board of directors in each of the twelve Federal Reserve Districts.

Even though these board members have little to do with the direct management of Fed employees, they do have some influence on the way the Fed operates. They approve salaries, review audit findings, provide guidance on interest rates, and approve major initiatives. As a result, they have some power over the Fed. They could possibly use this power to benefit the banking industry.

Limiting the influence member banks have on the Fed would reduce the bias of financial regulators and other Fed employees. This would help the Federal Reserve System to monitor and regulate more effectively America's financial system. A report by the Government Accountability Office released in October 2011 recommended "that the Federal Reserve Board encourage all Reserve Banks to consider ways to help enhance the economic and demographic diversity of perspectives on the boards, including by broadening their potential candidate pool."[105]

There is little reason to have bankers own stock in the Fed or nominate directors for the Fed's District banks. Even though the Fed assists in the banking industry, its primary focus should be to help the people of the United States.

Don't Allow Disregard for Regulation

Normally a law is passed and the regulators propose regulations to comply with the law. The proposed regulation has a public comment period where interested parties can comment on the proposed regulations. After the comment period, regulations are then finalized and enforced.

However, regulators can weakly enforce the regulations or issue guidance about how to comply with the regulations. This gives the regulators the flexibility to find ways to work around the existing and well-vetted regulations.

For example, in 2010, regulators gave bankers the advice to "pretend and extend." Bankers were given guidance by the regulators that allowed them to disregard valuation rules in extending loans. Normal regulations require that when banks make loans, the value of the collateral should exceed the amount of the loan. However, when property prices collapsed in 2010, bankers were told to pretend the value of loans was sufficient and extend the loan.

In 2010, the commercial real estate (CRE) market was under significant stress. As property values fell, more loans became delinquent, which made the market much riskier overall. The threat of CRE failure was particularly dire considering the enormous value, $1.8 trillion, of CRE loans held by banks in 2010.

In response to tremendous losses in the commercial real estate market, federal banking supervisors issued the Interagency Policy Statement on Prudent CRE Loan Workouts in October 2010. The purpose was to promote supervisory consistency, enhance the transparency of CRE workout transactions, and ensure that supervisory policies and actions did not inadvertently curtail the availability of credit to sound borrowers.[106] One part of the guidance was:

> "Understanding that restructured loans will not be adversely classified solely because the value of the underlying collateral has declined to an amount less than the loan balance."

In other words, the regulators were going to look the other way if banks disregarded their own policies on extending loans.

I believe that many more banks would have failed if this "pretend and extend" policy was not implemented. A large proportion of a commercial bank's assets are CRE loans. These banks would have incurred large losses if they had to foreclose on these loans. The resulting bank sell-off of foreclosed commercial properties would have further depressed property prices. This would begin a domino effect, causing even more foreclosures and more loan losses. This would have further restricted lending and caused the recession to be even worse.

That is why the regulators decided to implement "pretend and extend."[107] Many people look back and say this policy worked beautifully. The commercial real estate market slowly recovered over several years and these banks did not fail. We averted a worse recession.

However, this market incursion came at a cost to efficiency. This policy created a wedge between a buyer and seller's valuation of a building. The owner of a building with an existing loan valued it at a higher price than what a potential buyer would pay for it. As a result, the number of transactions plummeted. The reduction in sales volume negatively affected a lot of professionals in the commercial real estate value chain. These included real estate brokers, title companies, appraisers, local governments, and others that get a fee in a transaction. In addition, this caused rents to be higher than they otherwise would have been. Higher rents at the margin caused fewer employers to hire. So, the policy decreased economic activity. Investors who patiently waited with their stockpiles of cash to purchase distressed assets as a result of the binge lending and crash were disappointed.

Most importantly, the ad hoc change in policy slowed long-term growth because of a weakening of the rule of law. When regulators can change the rules on the fly to benefit the imprudent banks, the efficiency of the market is negatively affected.

Views from a Small Business Owner

An example of how this can play out are the thoughts of Wade Vitalis, a small business owner in Minnesota and Wisconsin who had to deal with banks during the downturn:

"I used to bank at the Central Bank of Florida, which expanded by buying distressed banks during the meltdown ... They were the ones during the Grantsburg expansion that bought the River Bank and gave me the green light on my expansion."

"The problem is all assets purchased from the FDIC had a term and loan commitment tied to security of the asset. If the business went under, the FDIC would cover most of the loss for the bank. But if the bank lent new money, they would be solely liable for that investment. While I realize that banks that bail out other banks are a net positive for the system overall in a situation like we were in, the FDIC terms simply gave the bank asset security, which gave them a further aversion to lend. Instead of punishing the TBTF [Too Big To Fail] shyster's on Wall Street that caused the problem, it hurt the businesses on Main Street."

"So, an unexpected consequence was that Central Bank took the security offered by the FDIC and then simply stopped lending to most of their business and consumer customers. Many businesses were in essence kicked out of the bank and left to fend for themselves in a very bank leery lending environment. I know this because I know a lot of those people that left. I am pretty sure there was a growth in assets of Credit Unions directly tied to the policy and the nature of the takeover of failing banks."[108]

In conclusion, banks are aided by the supervisors who regulate them. To reduce this conflict, regulators should hold higher capital, banks should not have any control over the regulators, and regulators should not be able to change the rules on-the-fly to benefit banks.

Part IV: Fed Favors the Rich

Chapter 10: Fed Makes the Rich Richer

"By some estimates, income and wealth inequality are near their highest levels in the past hundred years, much higher than the average during that time span and probably higher than for much of American history before then."
-Janet Yellen, Federal Reserve Chair

120

Americans had a collective wealth of $85 trillion in the first quarter of 2015.[109] However, this wealth is spread unevenly. Wealth is equal to a person's assets minus liabilities.

Every three years, the Fed conducts a Survey of Consumer Finance. This in-depth survey provides a cornucopia of detailed information on U.S. family finances, assets, and liabilities.

In 2013, the top ten percent of U.S. families owned 75 percent of the wealth. The bottom quarter owned negative 0.6; it was negative because the poor owed more than they owned.

Over the past 25 years, the range of wealth distribution has grown. In 1989, the top ten percent of families owned only 67 percent of the wealth. The bottom quarter owned just negative 0.1 percent.

In 2013, a family with net worth of more than $81,400 was in the top half of families in the U.S. If a family had more than $1,871,600, it was in the top 5 percent of all families. Also in 2013, the top ten percent of families owned 92 percent of the bonds, 77 percent of the stocks, and 58 percent of the retirement funds owned by American families.[110]

The Fed's monetary policy actions affect the value of wealth. Before I discuss the Fed's effect on the increasing inequality between America's richest and poorest citizens, I should point out that the Fed does not consider equality when conducting monetary policy. The Fed sets no goals related to economic inequality. A recent paper from the Philadelphia Fed discusses this topic and concludes that it is "probably impossible to avoid the redistributive consequences of [the Fed's] monetary policy."[111]

Matthew Kaul, Communications Director of MacLaurinCSF, said the question of inequality is one that the Fed needs to be aware of and contemplating, even if it doesn't necessarily change its mandate. However, he said the issue of inequality is intertwined with full employment and stable prices.[112]

Asset and liability values are affected by interest rates. Standard financial theory sets the present value of an asset or a liability equal to all discounted future cash flows. Future cash flows are discounted because future dollars are worth less than current dollars. The discount factor that is used is a form of an interest rate. This interest rate is affected by Fed monetary policy actions. In other words, today's value of an asset or liability equals the sum of all cash flows divided by the quantity of one plus interest rate raised to the power of time. Or, if you prefer the actual equation:

$$V = \Sigma(CF/(1 + i)^t)$$

Where V is today's value, Σ is summation, CF is cash flow, i is interest rate and t is a period in time.

Dividing a number by a large number results in a small number, while dividing a number by a small number results in a larger number. Therefore, a low interest rate results in an increased value.

To clarify, consider this example:

You are going to get paid $100 one year from now and another $100 two years from now. How much is that worth today?

The answer depends on the interest rate. Suppose you could get five percent interest by putting money into your local bank.

$95.24 = $\frac{\$100}{(1+.05)^1}$ This is today's value for 1st payment

$90.70 = $\frac{\$100}{(1+.05)^2}$ This is today's value for 2nd payment

The value of getting $100 one year from now and another $100 two years from now at a 5 percent interest rate is $185.94 = $95.24 + $90.70.

If you are still confused, think of it this way:

If you put $95.24 in a bank account that pays 5 percent interest, in one year you would have
$100 = $95.24 × 1.05

If you put $90.70 in a bank account that pays 5 percent interest you would get $100 in two years
($90.70 × 1.1025).

If the Interest Rate is Lowered, the Future Cash Flows are Valued More Today.

Suppose the interest rate is 2 percent. Then…

$98.04 $= \dfrac{\$100}{(1+.02)^{1}}$ This is today's value for 1st payment

$96.17 $= \dfrac{\$100}{(1+.02)^{2}}$ This is today's value for 2nd payment

The value of getting $100 one year from now and another $100 two years from now at a 2 percent interest rate is $194.16 = $98.02 + $96.17

Or you can think of it this way:

If you put $98.02 in a bank account that pays 2 percent interest. In one year you would have $100 = $98.02 × 1.02

If you put $96.17 in a bank account that pays 2 percent interest you would get $100 in two years ($96.17 × 1.0404).

To recap, by lowering the interest rate from 5 percent to 2 percent, the value of your future payments increased by $8.22 = $194.16 - $185.94 or 4.4 percent $\left(\dfrac{\$8.22}{\$185.94}\right)$.

The overall point is….

Lower Interest Rates Increase Values!

If you own assets, your values grow when interest rates decline.

America's rich own significantly more assets than the poor. When the value of rich people's assets increase, their wealth increases, making them wealthier.

Fortunately for the wealthy, the Federal Funds Rate has been very low in recent years (see Chart 6). The decrease in the Federal Funds Rate helps lower most interest rates and subsequently increases the value of assets like stocks (see Chart 7) and houses (see Chart 8).

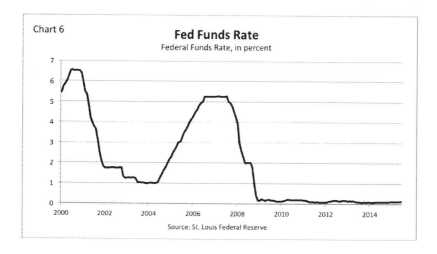

Chart 6

Fed Funds Rate

Federal Funds Rate, in percent

Source: St. Louis Federal Reserve

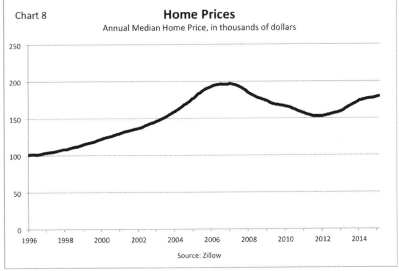

James Bullard, president of the St. Louis Fed, said he fears that maintaining low interest rates will create an asset bubble. "A risk of remaining at the zero lower bound too long is that a significant asset-market bubble will develop."[113] Bullard is further concerned with the Fed's historically poor ability to contain bubbles.

Former Federal Reserve board member Kevin Warsh described the Fed's monetary policy as "Robin Hood in reverse."[114] In other words, the policies benefit the rich while hurting the poor.

Monetary policy indirectly affects other things besides interest rates, like inflation and cash flows. Longer-term interest rates are affected by expected inflation. If the Fed lowers short-term rates, long-term rates could rise because of the inflation premium (discussed in Chapter 3). However, the Fed's recent monetary actions lowered both short and long-term rates because the Fed was purchasing long-term securities.

The Fed's monetary actions indirectly affect the overall economy. When the Fed lowers interest rates, it is cheaper to finance investments such as new buildings, bridges, coffee shops, employees, and startup companies. This increase in the real economy increases cash flows for a lot of people and companies. Therefore, lower interest rates benefit many people. This is why the Fed increases the supply of money, to stimulate the real economy.

Lower interest rates can also increase asset values by increasing future cash flows. This benefits the rich as well. When the rich obtain more wealth they consume some of it, but usually they invest more. This has a compounding effect on future wealth. When the Fed purchases bonds, which are mainly owned by the rich, the money received by the rich will be mainly invested. These investments can be put into other bonds, the stock market, property investments, investments in other countries, and other asset classes.

The rich get richer.

However, there is another tool that the Fed could use that would more make you better off, assuming that you are not in the top 1 percent on the wealth scale.

This tool has been talked about for centuries. Thomas Paine suggested it, Ben "Helicopter" Bernanke wrote about it, as did Milton Friedman[115].

If the Fed wants to create money out of thin air, it should not give it to the rich, it should give it to you!

Chapter 11: The Solution for You!

"It is well enough that people of the nation do not understand our banking and monetary system, for if they did, I believe there would be a revolution before tomorrow morning."
-Henry Ford, Businessman

The best way to describe the solution to the favor-the-rich regime is through a fictitious news article:

Federal Reserve Gives Everyone $10,000!

WASHINGTON - The U.S. Federal Reserve System gave $10,000 to every adult American citizen today in a surprise move to jumpstart the U.S. economy.

So far, it seems that the move has been well-received in every part of the country as evidenced by spontaneous mass celebrations.

"It's a godsend," said David Cole of Baltimore, MD. "This money is going to keep my family off the streets." Cole used his gift from the Fed to catch up on his rent.

Others used the money to pay down debts. "My sister-in-law finally paid me back for those Taylor Swift concert tickets." said John Weiss of Chicago, IL.

In a bold move, Federal Reserve chair, Megan Jones, ordered the transfer of funds known as the Service Acquisition of Consultants (SAC.) The SAC sent the electronic transactions using the Automated Clearing House service. The funds were transferred to bank accounts that are associated with social security numbers.

Many economists were surprised by the Fed's actions, including Former Fed Chairman Benjamin Stern. Stern earned the name "Helicopter Ben" for the theoretical paper he wrote which proposed distributing money as a monetary tool.

Part IV – Fed Favors the Rich

Many economists expect a spurt of inflation as a result of the Fed's move. "Inflation should rise about 2 percent this year," prophesied Cho Kim, an economist with Credit Co.

As more and more people began to spend their payout on goods and services, businesses raised prices in efforts to effectively distribute their supply. "I put a sign on the door that prices were 15 percent higher than marked, but people continued to stream into my store and buy my goods," said liquor store owner Christina Arndt.

The windfall also surprised Treasury officials.. The payments were technically fees paid to American "inflation consultants" and were treated as income. The Fed withheld the taxes from the payments and remitted $733.6 billion to the Treasury. This income tax revenue drastically reduced the Federal budget deficit and almost created a *budget surplus.*

Some people decided to save the payments. "After living paycheck to paycheck for so many years, it is nice to build some savings," said Jayden Downey.

Each American citizen with a social security number and a bank account received a payment from the Federal Reserve. Payments to others will be paid once their identity and social security number are verified.

Some U.S. Senators were upset by the Fed's move. "Fiscal policy decisions are reserved for Congress. We will be holding hearings to determine if the Fed overstepped its authority," said one senator. This comes down to a technicality as the Fed controls its own budget and can "hire" at will.

Some pundits suggested that this action may be the end for the Fed because Congress may act to weaken the authority of the Federal Reserve.

Chapter 11 - The Solution for You!

The European Central Bank was dumbfounded by the Fed's actions. "Citizens of European Union member countries are beginning to expect the same stimulus," said the EU bank president. "We will be analyzing the impact of the payments."

The increase in demand caught many companies flat-footed. Liquor store distributor JJ and Co is adding a third shift and numerous employees to its payroll in order to keep up with the added demand

"Take this job and shove it," said Kimmy Ortiz, who quit her job at Eagle Coal Mine. She plans to use her money to start her own business.

"I can't wait until the Fed does this again," says Jane, who lost all of her $10,000 at the River Bear Casino.

Some experts are concerned how the Fed's finances could handle this big payment. Under generally accepted accounting principles, payments to consultants are treated as an expense. This would create a huge loss on the Fed's income statement. However, the Fed uses its financial accounting manual that treats these payments as deferred assets. Therefore, the Fed's profits are not affected by the large cash payout.

Interest rates increased on longer term treasury bonds. The yield on the ten-year treasury is up by 37 basis points due to the inflation scare.

The governor of The People's Bank of China, which holds more than one trillion dollars in U.S. treasury bonds, expressed concern about the decreased prices. "China is extremely disappointed in the decision the United States made," the governor said.

Housing and mortgage activity picked up as a higher number of potential homebuyers have money for a down payment. Meanwhile, many others used the excess money to pay off their current mortgages.

Some of the transactions were rejected by member banks' fraud protection algorithms that noted huge numbers of transactions with the same dollar amounts. These rejections were quickly resolved after verification of the SAC program was officially announced on the Fed's website.

One consultant noted that the SAC could help the Fed reach its objectives to increase economic activity and raise inflation to the Fed's target of 2 percent. The consultant noted that the SAC did not increase inequality because everyone received the same payments.

"The beauty of the SAC is that it did not matter if you were rich or poor, employed or unemployed, war veteran, had more kids, invested or didn't invest, because everyone received the payment. People did not have to change their behavior to receive it," said analyst Maizie Caldwell of US Bancorp. "There was no change in incentives like there has been for other government tax and spending programs."

The S&P 500 index leapt 2 percent today due to higher sales expectations and more people investing their windfall into companies' stocks.

Some economists were concerned by the one-sided action. Under normal monetary policy, the Fed buys government bonds to increase the supply of money. To reduce the money supply the Fed can sell those bonds. However in this action, it will be difficult to reduce the supply of money in the future since they cannot ask for the money back.

Chapter 11 - The Solution for You!

Part IV – Fed Favors the Rich

Chapter 12: Watch Out for the Future

"It isn't so much that hard times are coming; the change observed is mostly soft times going." -
Groucho Marx, Comedian

Chapter 12 – Watch out for the Future

When the Fed raises interest rates, will the economy crash and burn?

The Federal Reserve has kept interest rates extremely low for an extended period of time. It also purchased trillions of dollars of Treasury and other government-backed bonds. The increased interest income from these bonds led to increased remittances from the Fed to the U.S. Treasury.

Eventually the Fed will "lift off" from low interest rates. When this happens, major changes will occur:

- The market value of the bonds that the Fed holds as assets will fall. This will create an insolvent Fed.
- The Treasury will receive smaller revenues from the Federal Reserve.
- The Fed will stop buying government debt and maybe even start selling bonds or let them mature.
- The Treasury will pay more interest expense on the new bonds it issues.

The lower revenues and increased expenses will put a squeeze on the government. This will be exacerbated by demographic changes of lower labor force growth and higher Social Security and Medicare payments.

Nobel Prize-winning economist Ed Prescott thinks a Fed rate hike and the resulting decrease in asset prices would greatly increase the deficit and "upset [Congress] something awful." "It's a scary thing," he said. [116]

"Congress is really scared of the Fed," he said. "We made $100 billion last year by borrowing short and lending long. Congress does not like not having control."

Congress will need to make tough decisions:

- Cut expenses
- Raise taxes
- Stop paying interest on debt
- Borrow even more at higher interest rates

The situation could become unsustainable with debt default, higher inflation, or severe austerity causing a recession.

Cutting expenses, raising taxes, or both, combined with higher interest rates, will reduce the overall demand for goods and services in the economy. These effects could be extreme enough to cause a depression.

The best outcome would be stagnation. Low labor force growth, a slow unwinding of the Fed's balance sheet, measured tax increases, budget cuts, and productivity gains could cause a long period of stagnation.

The International Monetary Fund issued a warning to the U.S. Federal Reserve that raising interest rates now could cause serious economic downturn.[117]

The Fed could also decide to postpone lift off, causing further inflation. Art Rolnick said he thinks a return to a two or three percent interest rate would only cause mild harm to the economy, in part because interest rates have often been around that rate in the past."[118]

Investor Fred Martin said he's concerned that when the Fed begins selling bonds, the bond market will face a liquidity crisis.[119]

Former Secretary of the Treasury Paulson is clearly worried about the future of America as he stated in his recent book:

"Debt is our number one enemy"

"Our long term fiscal situation is unsustainable"

"We must restore fiscal sanity to the way we manage our affairs and soon"

"The longer we delay the greater the reckoning will be"[120]

Afterword

"A wise man proportions his belief to the evidence"

-David Hume, Scottish Philosopher

Afterword

I hope you enjoyed reading this book and not only learned some important economic and financial concepts, but also expanded your knowledge on the Federal Reserve System and its impact on you.

This book is meant to provoke thought, educate, and inform. I hope that in reading this, you not only have gained knowledge about the Fed, but also will be asking questions. Question the way the Fed does things, and question my proposed solutions.

The Fed is not broken. It provides huge benefits to the United States and world economy. Despite this, the Fed is imperfect; it is fat, friendly to banks, and favors the rich. However, the cost of these imperfections is relatively small to the overall benefits the Fed provides.

As such, the solutions I provided are not risk-free. The implementation of the suggested solutions has the possibility of creating more costs and problems.

There are reasons why the Fed is the way it is. If a turnaround expert cuts muscle, rather than fat, the country could be worse off. If Congress decides to set the budget of the Fed, the Fed would lose some independence and the political influence would cause more costs to society than the cuts in the budget.

If the Fed became completely unfriendly to banks, rather than finding a balance, the country would be worse off. Banks provide important services of matching savers with borrowers. If the Fed were anti-bank, this important function could be impaired and people would have a harder time finding credit.

If the Fed sold all of its assets and gave them to all the American people, this would inhibit the ability of the Fed to reduce the money supply. In addition, inflation expectations could get out of control and the country could be worse off.

While the economy may be unstable, and there is always the possibility of recession, hyperinflation, or any other economic disaster, the American banking and financial system is one of the greatest in the world. Our system allows for innovation and advancements. The American Way has created huge improvements in the lives of everyday Americans, and there is one thing about which I am certain: because of our great system (despite its flaws), the average American will be better off twenty years from now he or she is today.

Appendix A: History of Banking and the Federal Reserve System

The American Revolution

During the American Revolution, paper money, called "Continentals," was produced. Continentals were denominated in "Dollars," which comes from the Spanish use of "Thalers," which originated hundreds of years earlier in the Czech town of Joachimsthal, where they produced a silver coin called Joachimsthalers – shortened to Thalers.

When the Second Continental Congress convened in Philadelphia during the height of the American Revolution, on May 10, 1775, it had no money in its treasury. Additionally, the British Navy essentially cut off all trade routes exiting the colonies. With no resources or international trade, the Second Continental Congress authorized the formation of Continental currency. On January 11, 1776, Congress resolved that should someone refuse to take the Continental currency notes as value equal to that of coin, that person should be "deemed, published, and treated as an enemy to his country." However, this form of fiat currency soon began to depreciate.

In January 1777, depreciation of the Continental currency was so great that Congress appealed to all states to make the money legal tender for public and private debts. Hyperinflation was partially caused by the British, who counterfeited the Continental currency and sent it over in ships in an effort to destroy American credit. Some states tried to regulate the price of goods and services in order to coincide with the hyperinflation of Continental currency, but citizens "violently denounced" the rising prices and constantly depreciating currency. On May 31, 1781, Continental bills ceased to circulate as money, by order of Congress.[121]

During the final decades of the 18th century, the United States had only three banks, but over 50 currencies in circulation.[122]

The First Central Bank of the United States

Early in the infancy of this country, there was no central bank. There was a great debate between Thomas Jefferson and Alexander Hamilton about the direction of American society and government. Jefferson advocated for small businesses, farmers, and more of an agrarian society, believing that there should not be a concentration of power in big banks and big businesses. Hamilton argued that there should be a strong national government with the ability to support international trade, large businesses, industrial organizations, and military. He also argued for easy funding of the federal government.[123]

In 1791, Thomas Jefferson wrote a letter to George Washington, detailing his argument against the bill proposed by Alexander Hamilton that would establish the national bank. He argued, "the incorporation of a bank, and the powers assumed by this bill, have not, in my opinion, been delegated to the U.S. by the Constitution." Jefferson's main point was that the powers given to the bank in the bill did not coincide with the "specially enumerated" powers written in the Constitution.[124]

Hamilton argued for the interests of commerce and industry, and argued the Bank's constitutionality on the grounds that the Federal Government may do something that is not explicitly prohibited and that may achieve a constitutional end.[125]

In 1791, Hamilton's arguments won and Congress chartered the first bank of the United States. The charter lasted for 20 years. This allowed for a more efficient and effective banking system, a funding source for the Treasury, and more order in official financial affairs. In 1811, after a very close vote, the charter was not renewed and was allowed to expire. The stock in the first bank was sold to a private enterprise.

The Second Central Bank of the United States

When the government had difficulties funding the war of 1812, Congress decided to re-charter the central bank, creating the Second Bank of the United States in 1816. The bank caused great controversy, facing two challenges to its constitutionality. However, in *McCulloch v. Maryland* (1819), the Supreme Court upheld the constitutionality of the bank in a 9-0 vote. In his opinion, Chief Justice Marshall wrote, "After the most deliberate consideration, it is the unanimous and decided opinion of this court that the act to incorporate the Bank of the United States is a law made in pursuance of the Constitution, and is part of the supreme law of the land."[126] The decision of the justices relied on the principle of enumerated powers and the supremacy granted to the Federal Government by the U.S. Constitution. This decision was later reaffirmed in *Osborn v. Bank of the United States* in 1824.[127]

The Second Bank was hindered by poor management and fraud. It wasn't until Nicholas Biddle became President of the Bank that it gained significant power. As the bank president, Biddle tried to use his power to influence politics. To do this, he used the central bank to lend money to various politicians while restricting political enemies and portions of the country access to credit. In essence, Biddle would try to create recessions in certain areas of the country, so that politicians in those areas would be perceived negatively.

The Bank War

The Second Bank provided the country with financial stability, and laid the foundation for a period of strong *economic growth*. Though Biddle had financial savvy and managerial skill, he was arrogant and unfamiliar with politics. Biddle thought his power was immense and that he could control the whole country, often going against Andrew Jackson, who was a vehement opponent of the central bank. Jackson believed it violated the constitutionally established principle of equality, placing economic favor on the wealthy. Jackson and Biddle's disagreement is known as the bank war.[128]

In 1832, before the charter for the Second Bank of the United States was set to expire, Congress drafted a bill to renew the bank's charter, but Jackson vetoed the bill. Biddle wasn't about to take it sitting down. He began a counterattack.

In August 1833, he started presenting state bank notes for redemption, calling in loans, and contracting credit every way he could. Biddle essentially tried to create a financial crisis, which he believed would convince people of the need for a central bank, and guarantee support for the renewal of the bank's charter in 1836.

The bank war became a hot-button issue for Congress and for the public. Business people, upset about difficult financial conditions, called for an end to the bank war one way or another. Biddle's opponents argued that his ability to influence the economy demonstrated the danger of a central bank. No new bills were drafted to renew the bank's charter, so, in 1836, the charter for the Second Bank of the United States expired.[129]

Multiple Currencies

After the second Bank of the United States, thousands of currencies were being circulated in the United States. Currency at this time was backed by specie, which allows for instant devaluation and recession because it relies on the value of the metal on a given day. The currency was highly varied; some had pictures of cows, and one even had a picture of Santa Claus. This made transactions difficult because if you were paid by somebody with a currency that was in a different state, backed by a bank, you didn't know if the bank was going to pay you the proper amount of gold if you presented it to them.

There was no way to compare the worth of one bank's currency to another. As such, there was a complex set of discounts where a dollar might be worth less than a dollar that was issued by a bank in a faraway location.[130]

Greenbacks

In 1862, Congress passed the Legal Tender Act, which authorized the creation of fiat money. This act issued $150 million of this new currency, called greenbacks, which was to be issued only by the federal government, and could be used as legal tender for payment of debts, public or private. However, paper bills issued by state banks still accounted for most of the currency in circulation.[131]

National Bank Act of 1863

Congress passed the National Bank Act of 1863 during the American Civil War to help relieve the financial crisis that had occurred earlier in the decade. To do so, the act created a national banking system, established a national currency, and floated federal war loans. The first provision of the act, creating a national banking system, allowed for the incorporation of banks. The national banks were similar to the state banks, the major difference being they received their charter from the federal government and not a state government. This allowed for greater control by the federal government over the banking system. The second provision, to create a national currency, minimized the possibility of counterfeits, and greatly simplified transactions. Now, rather than having thousands of currencies with unestablished values, there was one uniform currency, with an established value, that was accepted by all banks.

National Bank Act of 1864

The National Bank Act of 1864 added provisions to the National Bank Act of 1863. It allowed for the federal government to be active supervisors of commercial banks, establishing the Office of the Comptroller of the Currency.

In 1865, Congress added to the act, placing a 10 percent tax on state issued banknotes as an incentive for banks to join the national banking system.[132]

Boom Bust Cycles and Bank Panics of the 19th Century

The boom bust cycles of the 1800s were severe expansions and contractions in the *business cycle*. When people had faith in the banking industry, banks tended to be very generous with loans and people were eager to invest. Both the banks and people tended to overextend themselves, with people taking too much money out on loan and banks giving too much money for new projects. This phenomenon is known as the boom part of the cycle. When people discovered banks were lending out such significant amounts of money, they became concerned, wondering if they would be able to get their deposits back from the banks (remember - fractional banking). Panic would ensue as people rushed to the banks to get their money back. This is the bust part of the cycle. Banks had lent out the deposited money as loans to people, and couldn't give every customer back his or her full deposit. Because of this, banks would have to close, causing even more panic. This ultimately led to a recession or depression in the economy.

In their book *This Time is Different*, Carmen Reinhart and Kenneth Rogoff state that the economic crises from 1800-1913 were due to currency crashes, currency debasement, and inflation. A currency crash is defined as an annual depreciation against the U.S. dollar or other relevant anchor currency of fifteen percent or more. Currency debasement is defined as a reduction in the metallic content of coins in circulation of five percent or more. In this case, they define inflation as an annual inflation rate of twenty percent or more.[133]

Boom-bust cycles are cycles of economic expansion and contraction that occur repeatedly, and are often regarded as key characteristics of the modern capitalistic economy.

Panic of 1819

The culmination of the United States' first boom-to-bust economic cycle, the panic of 1819, was fueled by the vast land speculation that occurred in the years after the war of 1812. The Federal Government offered vast areas of land for sale. This land was easy for Americans to purchase because credit was easily available through the Second Bank of the United States. The number of banks in the United States more than doubled between 1812 and 1819. Many were chartered simply for the purpose of extending credit to land speculators.

These banks were unregulated, issuing excessive amounts of bank notes (promissory notes) that were not backed by gold or silver. So, credit was easily obtained by high-risk debtors. A global financial crisis emerged as banks suddenly began to restrict credit and call in loans. Poor management by the first bank president, William Jones, contributed to this becuse he allowed for the overextension of credit and then restricted credit too quickly. At the same time, the demand for American *exports* began to decrease as European production increased, causing a trade deficit in the United States. This triggered banks to declare bankruptcy because they did not have enough gold or silver to back the enormous amounts of promissory notes they had previously printed. In addition, many people lost their homes and farms because the banks quickly called for the repayment of loans, causing many foreclosures. This panic made evident the consequences of the lack of a national currency system that was regulated by a federal bank.[134]

Panic of 1837

A recession with bank failures, followed by a 5-year depression, the Panic of 1837 was a financial and economic crisis that occurred after the banking changes initiated by President Jackson and the specie circular. The specie circular required that paper banknotes no longer be accepted as payment for public lands, only gold and silver would be acceptable. Because of this, people began to rush to their banks to withdraw their funds. The panic began with a run on New

York City banks in May of 1837 and quickly spread throughout the nation.

Other causes include failure of the wheat crop, and a financial crisis in Great Britain. Unemployment and food riots hit the country, construction companies were unable to meet their obligations, and there were failures of bridges, roads, and canals.[135]

Panic of 1857

The Panic of 1857 came about after a period of overexpansion in the United States. The panic of 1857 was started by the closing of Cincinnati's Ohio Life Insurance and Trust Company. The New York branch of this bank closed in August of 1857, and the newly invented telegraph system quickly spread the news across the country. Panic ensued and people went to banks all around the nation to get their deposits. Land prices quickly fell, and the number of migrants decreased, causing financial problems for the railroad companies. Railroad companies that had over-expanded lost their value and went bankrupt.[136]

Panic of 1873

Jay Cooke and Company heavily invested in railroads. Soon, the firm found that it was unable to market the railroad bonds it had purchased. The firm realized it had overextended itself and declared bankruptcy. Many smaller banks did the same. Eighty-nine of the country's 364 railroads crashed into bankruptcy. A total of 18,000 businesses failed in a mere two years. By 1876, unemployment had risen to a frightening 14 percent."[137]

Panic of 1884

The panic of 1884 began when the brokerage house scam, operated by Ferdinand Ward and James Fish, collapsed. Instead of using the money to build new legs of the Erie Railroad, Ward and Fish used the money to speculate in the stock market. The firm ended up losing $27 million. A couple of days later, John Eno tried to escape to Canada with $4 million; he was not the only one. It turned out that the corruption had been widespread. Upon hearing this news, the public panicked. Luckily, the banks were able to act quickly to slow the panic, with J.P. Morgan acting as a lender of last resort.[138]

Panic of 1893

The panic of 1893 started with overbuilding and bad financing by the railroads, which resulted in a series of bank failures. A run on the gold supply compounded the issue. To pull out of the situation, President Grover Cleveland was forced to borrow $65 million from J.P. Morgan due to the depleted supply of gold in the United States Treasury. During this crisis, over 500 banks and 15,000 businesses closed. It was the worst economic downturn in United States history until this point in time.[139]

Panic of 1896

An acute recession, caused by a drop in silver reserves and market concerns about the effects it would have on the gold standard, the panic of 1896 was much smaller than other panics.[140].

Panic of 1907

The Panic of 1907 came about as a consequence of a crash in the stock price of the United Copper Company. The company's owner, F.A. Heinze, overreached himself in an attempt to corner the stock of the company. Heinze was president of Mercantile National Bank and had formed relationships with many other bankers to learn the business.[141]

While Heinze resigned from the bank, as did his associate C.W. Morse, the trouble did not end there. The New York Clearing House promised to help cover the withdrawals of customers of Mercantile National Bank. However, after learning that Charles T. Barney, the president of the Knickerbocker Trust Company, was a business associate of Heinze and Morse, many customers lined up to get their money back. Over $8 million was withdrawn in three hours, and the trust company closed early that afternoon. Customers were so desperate that people found paying jobs holding places in line. Panic spread and soon many other banks were forced to shut down as well.

The Panic of 1907 was particularly devastating. As a result, the country and economy suffered. Legislative leaders and financial moguls got together and tried to think of a solution to stop banking panics from happening. Consequently, the Pujo Committee was created. This Committee investigated "money trusts" of financial elites, such as J.P. Morgan.[142]

Creation of the Federal Reserve

In the aftermath of the panic of 1907, the Federal Reserve Act of 1913 was passed. This act created the Federal Reserve System, and granted it legal authority to create Federal Reserve Notes. In addition, it established twelve Federal Reserve Banks, each within a different economic province (*see map of districts*).

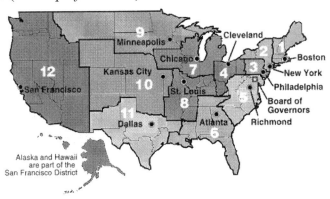

Source: Federal Reserve

The Federal Reserve is an independent central bank; its decisions do not have to be ratified by the President of the United States. However, the Fed is subject to oversight by Congress. While Congress does not micromanage the Fed's decisions, it ensures the Fed is working to achieve its objectives and not reaching far beyond its designated framework. The Fed can be thought of as "independent within the government."

The Board of Governors in Washington D.C. is a federal government agency. The board is composed of seven members who are appointed by the President of the United States and confirmed by the Senate. The full term for a member is 14 years. The Chairman and the Vice Chairman of the board are also appointed by the President and confirmed by the Senate. The Board of Governors supervises and regulates operation of each of the twelve District Banks, exercises broad responsibility in the nation's payments system, and administers most of the nation's laws regarding consumer credit protection. The board of governors has sole authority over changes in reserve requirements.

The Federal Reserve System is a network of twelve district banks. It carries out a variety of functions, including operating a nationwide payments system, distributing currency, supervising and regulating member banks, and serving as a banker for the U.S. Treasury. Each of the banks is responsible for its geographic area. The reserve banks also act as a depository for the banks in its own district.

Both the Board of Governors and the reserve banks work to supervise and regulate certain financial institutions and activities, provide banking services to depository institutions and the federal government, and ensure that consumers receive adequate information and fair treatment in their business with the banking system.

The voting members of the Federal Open Market Committee (FOMC) is made up of the members of the board of governors, the president of the Federal Reserve Bank of

New York, and the president of four other Federal Reserve banks, who serve on a rotating basis. The FOMC is responsible for overseeing open market operation, which is a tool used by the Fed to influence monetary and credit conditions.

Each of the reserve banks has its own board of directors, chosen from outside of the district bank management. They are meant to represent a variety of industries influenced by the actions of the district bank: commercial, agricultural, industrial, and public interests. The board of directors provides the Federal Reserve System with information on economic conditions throughout the country. The FOMC and board of governors use this information to make decisions regarding monetary policy[143]. (*See diagram of Federal Reserve structure and oversight*)

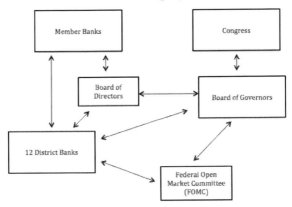

Federal Reserve structure and oversight

The Fed's currency is officially called Federal Reserve Notes. If you take a look in your pocket and pull out one of these green pieces of paper, you will notice the top of every one of them says, "Federal Reserve Note." Before 1933, these notes could be transferred for a bit of gold or silver at any local bank. However, we now use *fiat* money.[144]

The Great Depression

During the 1920s, many Americans were buying a considerable amount of goods, all on credit, and speculating in the stock market, creating rising debt. This pattern could not be sustained, and in 1929 the stock market crashed, triggering the Great Depression.

During the Great Depression, numerous banks failed. As a result, the money supply quickly contracted. Stuck with the gold standard, the central bank could not expand the money supply. In the early 1930s, the United States went off the gold standard for internal purposes. This was made in an attempt to increase liquidity[145].

Bretton Woods System

The 44 allied nations held a Financial and Monetary conference in 1944. Delegates from the 44 countries attended the conference to develop a plan for the world's financial future, using the experiences of the Great Depression and World War II to guide their discussions. One of the goals of the conference was to create stability in international exchange rates.

The Bretton Woods system established the International Monetary Fund (IMF), which holds funds from each country and serves as an emergency lender to all member countries.[146]

1970s and Stagflation

Prior to the 1970s, it was believed that there was a stable and inverse relationship between inflation and unemployment. It was believed that inflation was okay because it meant a growing economy and more jobs.

However, in the 1970s, *stagflation* occurred. Stagflation is the phenomenon marked by high unemployment as well as high inflation and low GDP growth. The observation of stagflation in the 1970s challenged the common belief that inflation and unemployment had a simple and predictable direct relationship.

To help curb unemployment and inflation, the Humphrey Hawkins Full Employment Act was passed, amending the earlier Employment Act of 1946. The Hawkins Act was similar to the Act of 1946, and named four ultimate goals: *full employment*, growth in production, price stability, and balance of trade and budget.[147]

Unlike the Employment Act of 1946, the Humphrey Hawkins Full Employment Act embraced *Keynesian theory,* in other words the idea that monetary policy can and should be used to stimulate *aggregate demand.* This idea is present in the Fed's operations today.

The goal of full employment was given priority over the goal of stable prices, as inflation continued to climb for several years. President Nixon put price controls in place to slow inflation. For a ninety-day period, wages and prices were frozen in order to combat inflation.[148] In 1974, President Ford revealed his "Whip Inflation Now" program, a.k.a. WIN, designed to curb inflation, which he called public enemy number one.

To reduce inflation, Paul Volcker – the chairman of the Fed at the time – began raising interest rates. At first, he raised them slowly, but eventually adopted a more aggressive approach.

Savings and Loan Crisis

The Savings and Loan (S&L) crisis began in the 1970s, with its peak in the 1980s, and finally came to an end in the 1990s. Because of the volatile interest rates in the 1970s, many depositors moved their funds from savings and loan institutions to money market funds. People did this because money market funds were not regulated by Regulation Q, which capped the amount of interest a bank could pay to depositors. "S&Ls, which were largely making their money from low-interest mortgages, did not have the means to offer higher interest rates, though they tried to once interest rate ceilings were dropped in the early 1980s. As S&L regulations loosened, they engaged in increasingly risky activities, including commercial real estate lending and investments in junk bonds."[149]

Check 21 Act

In the early 2000s, Congress created a law that allowed for an electronic image of a check to be a legal document. This is a very efficient payment option. An electronic transaction costs less than a penny to process, a paper check cost more than a dollar to process. About a quarter of the Fed's workforce was employed processing checks. This was part of the priced services area and required that the Fed recoup its costs and make a profit so it could compete against other private-sector operators.[150]

This law created a shift in the marketplace and a great reduction in the demand for check processing services because checks could now be processed electronically using image capture. As a priced service in a competitive environment, the Fed acted by closing numerous check processing centers and reducing the payroll in the check area tremendously. There is now only one check processing center, down from forty-five in 2003.[151]

2008 Financial Crisis

The 2008 financial crisis was caused in part by banks lending to those who are ill-qualified and unlikely to repay them. Loans given to borrowers with low credit are called *subprime loans*. These loans usually have very high interest rates. In my opinion, the large banks were "too big to fail" and therefore took on excessive risk. As borrowers began to default on their loans, numerous lending institutions became insolvent. The Fed responded by lowering the federal funds rate.[152]

Dodd-Frank Financial Wall Street Reform and Consumer Protection Act

Club Fed

The Dodd-Frank Act was passed by the Obama administration in 2010. This act was meant to protect against the reoccurrence of the events that caused the financial crisis in 2008. The act established new government agencies to monitor the performance of companies previously thought of as "too big to fail."[153]

Appendix B: Examples of District Bank Research and Programs

This appendix provides examples of research and programs funded by the Fed's 12 District Banks. Each District Bank's duties are essentially the same, but operations can vary from district to district. Some differences may be attributed to the differences among the regions each bank represents, while others come from differences in the priorities of each bank's management. This appendix includes examples of spending I believe to be extraneous to the Fed's core mission. However, the loose nature of the Fed's directives leaves things up in the air.

Brief information about each bank is provided, including the bank's 2014 operating expenses, total number of employees, and efficiency rating among the world's central banks, according to a study done by the Central Bank of Colombia.

Atlanta Fed

Operating Expenses: $642 million[154]
Employees: 1,586[155]
Central Bank Efficiency Ranking: 10th[156]

6–F

ATLANTA [157]

Appendix B – Examples of District Bank Research and
Programs

The Federal Reserve Bank of Atlanta is responsible for the Sixth Federal Reserve District, and covers the states of Alabama, Florida, and Georgia, and portions of Louisiana, Mississippi, and Tennessee. This District has offices in Atlanta, Birmingham, Jacksonville, Miami, Nashville, and New Orleans.

Like the other Districts, the Atlanta Fed spends money on programs that help the region's banks better serve their communities. These programs include research, publications, and community education.

For example, the research paper titled, "Do Minimum Wages Really Increase Youth Drinking and Drunk Driving?" written by M. Melinda Pitts in collaboration with economists Joseph J. Sabia and Laura Argys, references a study that found a positive correlation between minimum wage increases and youth (age 16-20) drunk driving fatalities. However, the study found "little evidence that an increase in the minimum wage leads to increases in alcohol consumption or drunk driving among teenagers."[158]

In addition, M. Melinda Pitts, an Atlanta Federal Reserve economist, is the director of the Center for *Human Capital* Studies[159] at the Atlanta Fed. According to the Center's webpage, "the Atlanta Fed has a natural interest in deepening its understanding of labor force dynamics and workforce development issues. The Center for Human Capital Studies supports those efforts through its research, as well as by offering such resources as conferences, seminars, and labor market tracking tools."

Another example is the research paper, "Social Ties, Space, and Resilience: Literature Review of Community Resilience to Disasters and Constituent Social and Built Environment Factors," written by Atlanta Fed research analyst Ann Carpenter. The paper describes the link between the strength of social networks and the resilience of communities following natural disasters. In the words of the author, "this literature review examines evidence linking strong social networks, a varied and integrated built environment, and greater resilience." The paper concludes that strong social networks lead to greater resilience in communities, and that the built environment also contributes to resilience by encouraging and supporting strong social networks.[160]

The Atlanta Fed hosted an event free of charge at a luxury hotel and resort on a renowned golf course for the lesson: "Broke: Financial Lessons from Athletes." The event was to caution students about the financial problems celebrity athletes face. The website says: "Many students aspire to be professional athletes, lured by the promise of fame and mega salaries. Yet what they may not know is that 60 percent of former NBA players are broke within five years of retirement and that 78 percent of former NFL players have gone bankrupt or are under financial stress within two years of leaving the league."[161]

Boston Fed

Operating Expenses: $325 million[162]
Employees: 1,072[163]
Central Bank Efficiency Ranking: 25[164]

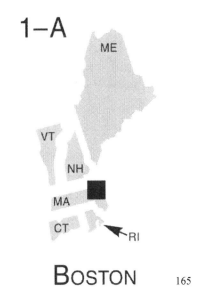

1-A

BOSTON [165]

The Federal Reserve Bank of Boston is responsible for the First Federal Reserve District, which covers the states of Connecticut, Massachusetts, Maine, New Hampshire, Rhode Island, and Vermont.

Like the other Districts, the Boston Fed spends money on numerous projects. This includes research publications, and programs that promote community betterment.

An example is, "Enforcement and Immigrant Location Choice,"[166] written by Boston Fed economist Tara Watson. According to the author, "this paper investigates the effect of local immigration enforcement regimes on the migration decisions of the foreign-born." Specifically, the paper examines the effects of the Delegation of Immigration Authority Section 287(g) Immigration and Nationality Act, which allows state or local law enforcement to enforce Federal immigration law. While it may be true that immigrants make up a large section of the workforce, the paper focuses primarily on whether or not 287(g) influences immigrants to leave the United States or deters them from entering.

"Window Shopping,"[167] written by Boston Fed economist Oz Shy, focuses on the economics of window shopping. Window shopping is "the activity in which potential buyers visit a brick-and-mortar store to examine a product but end up either not buying it or buying the product from an online retailer." This relates to understanding consumer preferences and *microeconomics.*

Similar to other Federal Reserve Banks, the Federal Reserve Bank of Boston's website has an entire section devoted to "Community Development," with the objectives:

Appendix B – Examples of District Bank Research and Programs

1. Strengthen the prospects of smaller cities in New England
2. Promote household financial stability
3. Increase community development lending
4. Promote equal access to housing resources[168]

Chicago Fed

Operating Expenses: $449 million[169]
Employees: 1,502[170]
Central Bank Efficiency Ranking: 15[171]

7–G

CHICAGO   172

169

Appendix B – Examples of District Bank Research and Programs

The Federal Reserve Bank of Chicago is responsible for the Seventh Federal Reserve District, encompassing the northern half of Illinois, southern half of Wisconsin, Iowa, Indiana, and Michigan's lower peninsula. The Chicago Fed has a branch in Detroit.

Similar to other Federal Reserve Banks, the Chicago Fed invests its resources in research, programs, and events. The research paper, "Saving Europe?" written by Chicago Fed economists Enrique G. Mendoza, Linda L. Tesar, and Jing Zhang. This paper focuses on analysis of European data to show that "unilateral capital tax increases cannot restore fiscal solvency,"[173] which relates to fiscal policy.

Another example is "Early Life Environment and Racial Inequality in Education and Earnings in the United States," by Chicago Fed economists Kenneth Y. Chay, Jonathan Guryan, and Bhash Mazumder. The authors describe their publication: "This study analyzes whether the across-cohort patterns in the black-white education and earnings gaps match those in early life health and test scores already established" The results of this publication shows, "a significant narrowing across the same cohorts in education gaps driven primarily by a relative increase in the probability of blacks going to college," and, "a similar convergence in relative earnings that is insensitive to adjustments for employment selection."[174]

Cleveland Fed

Operating Expenses: $302 Million[175]
Employees: 946[176]
Central Bank Efficiency Ranking: 19[177]

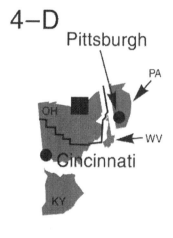

CLEVELAND   178

171

Appendix B – Examples of District Bank Research and Programs

The Federal Reserve Bank of Cleveland is the headquarters of the Fourth Federal Reserve District, which encompasses the entire state of Ohio, eastern Kentucky, western Pennsylvania and a small part of West Virginia. The Cleveland Fed has branches in the cities of Cincinnati and Pittsburgh.

An example of research in the Cleveland Fed that doesn't have much to do with the Federal Reserve's core objectives is a paper by Peter Hinrich, "What Kind of Teacher are Schools Looking For? Evidence from a Randomized Field Experiment." The author conducted an experiment by sending schools fake resumes with randomly chosen characteristics to determine which characteristics schools value when evaluating applicants. According to the study, the academic background of the applicant has little impact on hiring in private and charter schools, but private schools prefer applicants from more selective colleges. Private schools tended to have a slight preference towards female candidates, and all three sectors of schools preferred in-state applicants.[179]

Another example of extraneous research done by the Cleveland Fed is the study "Demographic Changes in and near US Downtowns," done by Nathaniel Baum-Snow and Daniel Hartley. The study tracked the demographic makeup of people who have lived near the downtown areas of major U.S. cities since 1970.

The study found that the overall population near downtowns declined in number, and in average income

172

between 1970 and 1980, but both have risen since then, especially in the period between 2000 and 2010.[180]

*Appendix B – Examples of District Bank Research and
Programs*

Dallas Fed

Operating Expenses: $291 million[181]
Employees: 1,243[182]
Central Bank Efficiency Ranking: 29[183]

DALLAS   184

The Federal Reserve Bank of Dallas is responsible for the Eleventh Federal Reserve District, which encompasses the entire state of Texas, northern Louisiana, and southern New Mexico. The Dallas Fed has branches in the cities of Houston, San Antonio, and El Paso.

The Federal Reserve Bank of Dallas also engages in Fed-funded research and activities. For example, the research publication, *Crossroads—Economic trends of the Desert Southwest*, published by the El Paso branch of the Dallas Fed. In the 2014 issue of *Crossroads*, Dallas Fed economist Roberto Coronado writes, in partnership with Marycruz de Leon, the article, "Tourism and Recreation a Bright Spot in the Big Bend Region." The authors provide an abstract of the article, "Although challenges exist for the Big Bend region, bullish cattle prices, Mexico's reforms, the energy boom in the Permian Basin, and a stronger U.S. economy, all bode well for the tri-county area."[185]

Appendix B – Examples of District Bank Research and Programs

Kansas City Fed

Operating Expenses: $256 million[186]
Employees: 1,528[187]
Central Bank Efficiency Ranking: 22[188]

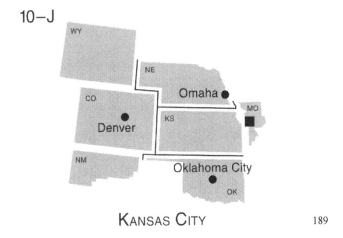

Kansas City   189

176

The Federal Reserve of Kansas City is responsible for the Tenth Federal Reserve District, which encompasses the western half of Missouri, Oklahoma, Kansas, the northern half of New Mexico, Colorado, Nebraska, and Wyoming. The Kansas City Fed also has branches in Denver, Omaha, and Oklahoma City.

An example of research from the Kansas City Fed is the paper "Student Loans: Overview and Issues," written by Kansas City Fed economists Kelly D. Edmiston and Steven Shepelwich in collaboration with Lara Brooks from Oklahoma State University. The abstract states: "This paper provides a detailed overview of the student loan market, presents new statistics that highlight student loan debt burdens and delinquency rates, and discusses current concerns among many Americans about student loans, including their fiscal impact ... the report is intended to enhance awareness of the state of student loan debt and delinquency."[190]

Another article by Kelly D. Edmiston is the research paper "Nonprofit Housing Investment and Local Area Home Values." She states in her paper that, "This article explores the impact of [community development corporations] housing investments in [low or moderate income] neighborhoods on neighborhood quality by estimating the effect of that investment on the value of nearby houses."[191]

Appendix B – Examples of District Bank Research and Programs

Minneapolis Fed

Operating Expenses: $214 million[192]
Employees: 1,097[193]
Central Bank Efficiency Ranking: 20[194]

9–1

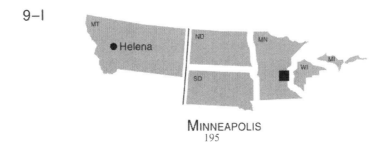

MINNEAPOLIS
195

178

The Federal Reserve Bank of Minneapolis oversees the Ninth Federal Reserve District. The Ninth District encompasses Minnesota, northern Wisconsin, Michigan's upper peninsula, North and South Dakota, and Montana. It also has a branch in Helena, Montana.

The Minneapolis Fed publishes the *fedgazette*, a regional business and economics newspaper. One article in the publication is titled "Organize it, and they will come?"[196] written by Ronald A. Wirtz. The article analyzes the effects of volunteer labor in non-profit organizations. It focuses on changes in volunteerism in the Ninth District states.

Research papers are also published by the Minneapolis Fed. The economic policy paper "Taxing Wealth," written by consultant Ellen R. McGrattan, examines the effects of wealth taxation. The results of the paper "aren't yet able to provide accurate predictions on the impact of wealth taxation."[197]

The research publication, "How Rich Will China Become?" written by research analyst Jingyi Jiang and special policy advisor to the president, Kei-Mu Yi, sets about to "provide a suggestive calculation for China's future per capita income."[198]

The Minneapolis Fed also operates a "Center for Indian Country Development." According to the Minneapolis Fed, "our emphasis is on helping tribes build governance, infrastructure, financial access, and resources to support sustainable business development in Native communities."[199]

Appendix B – Examples of District Bank Research and Programs

New York Fed

Operating Expenses: $1,818 million[200]
Employees: 3,225[201]
Central Bank Efficiency Ranking: 16[202]

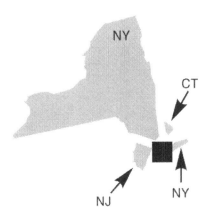

NEW YORK [203]

The Federal Reserve Bank of New York controls the Second Federal Reserve District system. The Second District includes New York, northern New Jersey, and part of Connecticut, Puerto Rico, and the U.S. Virgin Islands. It is the largest of the Federal Reserve Banks as measured by assets.

180

A research paper called "Are Recent College Graduates Finding Good Jobs?" was written by economists Jaison R. Abel, Richard Deitz, and Yaquin Su. This paper takes a look at employment outcomes for new college graduates over the last two decades. Many people thought that the Great Recession was responsible for the struggle new college graduates were having when it came to finding a good job. According to the data, individuals just beginning their careers often take time to meld into the job market. However, there are now more people who are unemployed or underemployed. Underemployment is when a college graduate works at a job that usually does not require a bachelor's degree. This percentage has risen sharply since the 2001 recession. In addition, the quality of employment that the underemployed do find has deteriorated. The new graduates of today are taking low-paying jobs or working part-time more and more often.[204]

Another research paper, also written by Jaison R. Abel and Richard Deitz, called "The Causes and Consequences of Puerto Rico's Declining Population," looks at the drop in the population of Puerto Rico over the last ten years. The rate of decline in the population of Puerto Rico has increased in recent years. Part of this drop is because of a slowdown in the birth rate, but the major factor has been a sudden exodus of its populace. The article suggests that to counter this outflux of people it must expand employment opportunities and solidify its economy.[205]

"Do the Benefits of College Still Outweigh the Costs?" looks at whether or not a college degree is still a good investment in the wake of rising tuition costs with many college students earning less upon graduation. This article was also written by Jaison R. Abel and Richard Deitz. It finds that for both a bachelor's degree and an associate's degree, the benefits outweigh the costs. Both degrees provide about a fifteen percent return on investment.[206]

Philadelphia Fed

Operating Expenses: $322 million[207]
Employees: 942[208]
Central Bank Efficiency Ranking: 17[209]

3-C

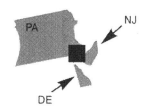

PHILADELPHIA ₂₁₀

Appendix B – Examples of District Bank Research and Programs

The Federal Reserve Bank of Philadelphia oversees the Third Federal Reserve district, the physically smallest in the Federal Reserve System. It covers the eastern half of Pennsylvania, the southern part of New Jersey and the entirety of Delaware. Even though it is by far the smallest geographically, it is only the second smallest by population, beating out the Minneapolis district.

One research project at the Philadelphia Federal Reserve is "History and the Sizes of Cities" by Hoyt Bleakley and Jeffrey Lin. In this paper, they look at some commonly used models for determining the growth of a city and they determine that it is inconsistent with the data. They also suggest several modifications to the model that might allow it to be consistent with the historical data.[211]

Another research paper is "Weather-Adjusting Employment Data" by Michael Boldin from the Fed and Jonathan H. Wright from Johns Hopkins University. In this paper, the authors propose and use a statistical model to adjust employment data for the deviation of weather patterns from what is normal for the season. They used a number of statistics for weather, including temperature, snowfall, and hurricanes. According to the paper, they found that weather has a huge effect. It can cause the payroll to shift by over $100,000 in either direction. The research found that the effects are largest in the winter and early spring months, and that the construction industry was the most affected.[212]

A third research project is "Identity Theft as a Teachable Moment" by Julia Cheney, Robert Hunt, Vyacheslav Mikhed, Dubravska Ritter, and Michael Vogan. In this project, they looked at how cases of identity theft that are bad enough to cause people to place a fraud alert in their credit reports affect their risk scores, delinquencies, and other credit bureau variables on impact and thereafter. For a great many people, these effects are small and temporary. That being said, a significant number of people, especially those who tended to have lower risk scores before their identities were stolen, had long-lasting positive effects on their credit bureau variables. They conclude that this is because the consumer gets more information on their credit file.[213]

Another research paper is titled "Partisan Conflict," by Marina Azzimonti. In this article, she finds that an increase in partisan conflict has a negative impact on the government's policy in regard to the economy. Especially harmful are the periodic government shutdowns that are a result of such incapability to work together. The author finds that an increase in partisan conflict increases government deficits and significantly discourages investment, output, and employment.[214]

Appendix B – Examples of District Bank Research and Programs

Richmond

Operating Expenses: $667 million[215]
Employees: 1,563[216]
Central Bank Efficiency Ranking: 26[217]

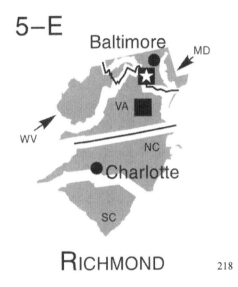

RICHMOND   218

186

The Federal Reserve Bank of Richmond is responsible for the Fifth Federal Reserve District, which covers South Carolina, North Carolina, Virginia, most of West Virginia, the District of Columbia, and Maryland. It has branches in Baltimore and Charlotte.

One example of research in Richmond that has nothing to do with the core mission of the Federal Reserve System is the paper "Learning and Life Cycle Patterns of Occupational Transitions." This paper, written by Aspen Gorry, Devon Gorry, and Nicholas Trachter, shows that over forty percent of high school graduates switch between white collar and blue collar jobs multiple times between the ages of eighteen and twenty eight. Using the data available, the authors have developed a model based on workers sorting themselves to the job that is the best match for them. Initial characteristics can predict future job switching patterns. The patterns included by the model include the timing of each switch and the number of switches.[219]

Appendix B – Examples of District Bank Research and Programs

San Francisco Fed

Operating Expenses: $630 million[220]
Employees: 1,667[221]
Central Bank Efficiency Ranking: 13[222]

SAN FRANCISCO   223

The Federal Reserve Bank of San Francisco is the headquarters of the Twelfth Federal Reserve District, which covers the states of California, Washington, Oregon, Idaho, Nevada, Utah, Arizona, Alaska, and Hawaii. It has branches in Los Angeles, Portland, Salt Lake City, and Seattle.

The San Francisco branch of the Fed is the largest in terms of area and population, and the second-largest by assets held after New York. As such, they have the capital to move forward and do enormous amounts of research and community education that may or may not align with the Fed's mission.

One example of research at the San Francisco Federal Reserve is a paper entitled "Does Medicare Part D save Lives?" by Abe Dunn and Adam Hale Shapiro. Medicare Part D was created with the aim of reducing the burden of drug expenditures for the elderly. The finding was that between 19,000 and 27,000 individuals were alive in mid-2007 because of the Part D implementation in 2006. This research shows the effectiveness of a government program.[224]

Another example of research conducted at the Federal Reserve Bank of San Francisco is "The Changing Role of Disabled Children Benefits" by Richard V. Burkhauser and Mary C. Daly. This research takes a look at the expenditures of the government's Supplemental Security Income program for disabled children, which provides money to low-income families that have a disabled child. When the program was established in 1974, there were about 71,000 disabled children receiving the benefits for a total cost of forty million dollars. Since then, the program has grown to 1.3 million children and costs over nine billion dollars. The research explores the fact that the increase in enrollment is not due to an increase in families who qualify based on income, nor an increase in the number of disabled children. Instead, the rise was likely caused by the relaxing of admittance requirements and the interpretation by Social Security evaluators.[225]

According to research by William Dowling, children born into poverty face many effects that follow them their whole lives. These effects include working fewer hours, earning a much smaller income, and a heavier reliance on food stamps. In addition, children born well above the poverty line complete an average of two extra years in school and have a reduced risk of adulthood obesity. The report notes that just an increase of $3,000 in parental income between the time a child is born and its fifth birthday can provide a 19 percent increase in adult income.[226]

St. Louis Fed

Operating Expenses: \$318 Million[227]
Employees: 1,146[228]
Central Bank Efficiency Ranking: 9[229]

8–H

ST. LOUIS 230

191

Appendix B – Examples of District Bank Research and
Programs

The Federal Reserve Bank of St. Louis is the headquarters of the Eighth Federal Reserve District, which covers the eastern half of Missouri, Arkansas, southern Illinois, southern Indiana, western Kentucky, western Tennessee, and northern Mississippi. It also has branches in Little Rock, Louisville, and Memphis.

The Federal Reserve Bank of St. Louis conducts many different research projects and is also involved in the community.

One example of research is a paper by John Knowles and Guillaume Vandenbroucke, "Fertility Shocks and Equilibrium Marriage-Rate Dynamics." This paper explores the finding that when an event such as a war dramatically alters the male to female ratio, marriage probability, somewhat counterintuitively, actually increases. The main example of this that they use is France in World War I. After the war, the number of single men per single women was forty percent below the pre-war average. However, despite this poor male to female ratio, marriage rates actually increased by 47 percent for young women and 114 percent for older women.[231]

Another example is a paper entitled "Schools and Stimulus," by William Dupor and M. Saif Mehkari. This paper analyzes the impact of the education funding component of the American Recovery and Reinvestment Act from 2009. They estimate that out of one million dollars, fifty-seven percent of the money was used on expenditures, while employment in the district changed little, "and an additional $370 thousand in debt was accumulated." Seventy percent of the increase in spending was used for capital overlays. This is money spent to obtain, maintain, or repair things such as land, facilities, and machinery. From this data, they were able to build a model of a school district's budget problem, which they can adjust using the staffing levels and expenditure of each individual school district.[232]

The Federal Reserve Bank of St. Louis also runs the Center for Household Financial Stability, founded in May of 2013 to research and strengthen the balance sheets of struggling families. The Center organizes research, policy, and community forums locally and nationwide to understand better and respond to the balance-sheet issues affecting struggling families and communities.[233]

Board of Governors

Operating Expenses: $597 million[234]
Employees: 2,648[235]
Central Bank Efficiency Ranking: 2[236]

Like all of the other banks in the Federal Reserve System, the Board of Governors also invests in research.

For example, there is a paper by Jenny Schuetz called "Why are Wal-Mart and Target Next-Door Neighbors?" It takes a look at how big-box stores such as Target and Wal-Mart choose locations. The author hypothesizes that big-box stores would seek to establish spatial monopolies far from competitors due to the fact that they compete mainly on price while selling many of the same products. However, the results appear to show that while they tend to locate near complementary stores and far away from other stores of the same company, there is little evidence to show that the big-box stores try to locate new stores farther from competitors. The author suggests that this could be because stores would rather share customers in a good location than surrender the whole market to competitors.[237]

In another fascinating, albeit possibly unrelated, study, "Returning to the Nest: Debt and Parental Co-residence Among Young Adults," Lisa J. Dettling and Joanne W. Hsu take a look at the relationship between the indebtedness of a young adult and the decision to move back in with his or her parents. They found that indebtedness "increases flows into

194

parental co-residence." In addition, they found that young adults with low credit scores and delinquency tend to spend a longer time living with their parents after returning.[238]

Glossary of Terms

A

Aggregate Demand

"Aggregate demand (AD) is the total demand by domestic and foreign households and firms for an economy's scarce resources, less the demand by domestic households and firms for resources from abroad."[239]

Appreciation

"An increase in the value of an asset over time."[240]

Asset

"An asset of an individual or business firm is an item of value that the individual or firm owns."[241]

B

Balance Sheet

"A statement of the assets, liabilities and net worth of a firm or individual at some given time."[242]

Bond

"A certificate of indebtedness."[243]

Budget Deficit

"A shortfall of tax revenue from government spending."[244]

Budget Surplus

"An excess of tax revenue over government spending."[245]

Business Cycle

"Fluctuations in economic activity such as employment and production."[246]

C

Capital

See equity

Capital Ratio

"A measurement of a company's financial leverage, calculated as the company's debt, divided by its total capital."[247]

Central Bank

"An institution designed to oversee the banking system and regulate the quantity of money in the economy."[248]

Collateral

"Property or other assets that a borrower offers a lender to secure a loan."[249]

Collective Bargaining

"The process by which unions and firms agree on the terms of employment."[250]

Commodity

"A commodity is a marketable item produced to satisfy wants or needs."[251]

Commodity Money

"Money that takes the form of a commodity with intrinsic value."[252]

Competition

"Rivalry in which every seller tries to get what other sellers are seeking at the same time: sales, profit, and market share, by offering the best practicable combination of price, quality, and service. Where the market information flows freely, competition plays a regulatory function in balancing demand and supply."[253]

Complements

"Two goods for which an increase in the price of one leads to a decrease in demand for the other."[254]

Compounding

"The accumulation of a sum of money in, say, a bank account where the interest earned remains in the account to earn additional interest in the future."[255]

Consumer Price Index

"A measure of the overall cost of the goods and services bought by a typical consumer."[256]

Cost

"The value of everything a seller must give up to produce a good."[257].

Currency

"The paper bills and coins in the hands of the public."[258]

Cyclical Unemployment

"The deviation of unemployment from its natural rate."[259]

D

Decision Making

"Comparing the additional costs of alternatives with the additional benefits. Many choices involve doing a little more or a little less of something: few choices are 'all or nothing' decisions."[260]

Demand

"Demand refers to how much (quantity) of a product or service is desired by buyers. The quantity demanded is the amount of a product people are willing to buy at a certain price."[261]

Demand Deposits

"Balances in bank accounts that depositors can access on demand by writing a check."[262].

Demand Curve

"A graph of the relationship between the price of a good and the quantity demanded."[263]

Depreciation

"A decrease in an asset's value caused by unfavorable market conditions."[264]

Depression

"A severe recession."[265]

Diminishing Returns

"The property whereby the benefit from an extra unit of an input declines as the quantity of the input increases."[266]

Discount Rate

"The interest rate on loans that the Fed makes to banks."[267]

Diversification

"The reduction of risk achieved by replacing a single risk with a large number of smaller unrelated risks."[268]

E

Economics

"The study of how society manages its scarce resources."[269]

Economic Growth

"Investment in factories, machinery, new technology, and in the health, education, and training of people stimulates economic growth and can raise future standards of living."[270]

Economies of Scale

"The forces which reduce the Average cost of producing a product as the firm expands the size of its output in the long run."[271]

Efficiency

"The property of society getting the most it can from its scarce resources."[272]

Elasticity

"A measure of the responsiveness of quantity demanded or quantity supplied to one of its determinants."[273]

Entrepreneurship

"Entrepreneurs take on the calculated risk of starting new businesses, either by embarking on new ventures similar to existing ones or by introducing new innovations. Entrepreneurial innovation is an important source of economic growth."[274]

Equilibrium

"A situation in which the price has reached the level where quantity supplied equals quantity demanded."[275]

Equilibrium Price

"The price that balances quantity supplied and quantity demanded."[276]

Equilibrium Quantity

"The quantity supplied and the quantity demanded at the equilibrium price."[277]

Equity

"Assets minus liabilities."[278]

Exchange Rate

"Real exchange rate: the rate at which a person can trade the goods and services of one country for the goods and services of another."[279]

Exports

"Goods produced domestically and sold abroad."[280]

Externality

"An externality exists when the actions of a specified group of economic agents have significant economic repercussions on agents outside the group."[281]

F

Federal Deposit Insurance Corporation (FDIC)
"The federally chartered corporation which insures the deposit liabilities of commercial banks and thrift institutions."[282]

Federal Open Market Committee
"The Federal Reserve controls the three tools of monetary policy--open market operations, the discount rate, and reserve requirements. The Board of Governors of the Federal Reserve System is responsible for the discount rate and reserve requirements, and the Federal Open Market Committee is responsible for open market operations. Using the three tools, the Federal Reserve influences the demand for, and supply of, balances that depository institutions hold at Federal Reserve Banks and in this way alters the federal funds rate. The federal funds rate is the interest rate at which depository institutions lend balances at the Federal Reserve to other depository institutions overnight."[283]

Federal Reserve
"The central bank of the United States."[284]

Fiat Money
"Money without intrinsic value that is used as money because of government decree."[285]

Financial Intermediaries
"Financial institutions through which savers can indirectly provide funds to borrowers."[286]

Financial Markets
"Broad term describing any marketplace where buyers and sellers participate in the trade of assets such as equities, bonds, currencies and derivatives. Financial markets are

typically defined by having transparent pricing, basic regulations on trading, costs and fees and market forces determining the prices of securities that trade."[287]

Fiscal Policy
"Changes in government spending and tax collections."[288]

Fractional Reserve Banking
"A banking system in which banks hold only a fraction of deposits as reserves."[289]

Free-rider problem
"In economics, the free- rider problem refers to a situation where some individuals in a population either consume more than their fair share of a common resource, or pay less than their fair share of the cost of a common resource."[290]

Frictional Unemployment
"Unemployment that results because it takes time for workers to search for the jobs that best suit their tastes and skills."[291]

Full Employment
"Using all available resources to produce goods and services."[292]

Full Reserve Banking
"If someone puts money in their demand deposit account, the bank has to keep it there."[293]

Future Value
"The amount of money in the future that an amount of money today will yield, given prevailing interest rates."[294]

G

GDP Deflator
"A measure of the price level calculated as the ratio of nominal GDP to real GDP times 100."[295]

Gold Standard

"The gold standard was a commitment by participating countries to fix the prices of their domestic currencies in terms of a specified amount of gold."[296]

H

Human Capital

"The collective skills, knowledge, or other intangible assets of individuals that can be used to create economic value for the individuals, their employers, or their community."[297]

Hyperinflation

"A very rapid rise in the price level."[298]

I

Incentive

"Something that encourages a person to do something or to work harder."[299]

Imports

"Goods produced abroad and sold domestically."[300]

Institutions

"Institutions evolve and are created to help individuals and groups accomplish their goals. Banks, labor unions, markets, corporations, legal systems, and not-for-profit organizations are examples of important institutions. A different kind of institution, clearly defined and enforced property rights, is essential to a market economy."[301]

Income

"Income for most people is determined by the market value of the productive resources they sell. What workers earn primarily depends on the market value of what they produce."[302]

Inflation

"An increase in the overall level of prices in the economy."[303]

Inflation Tax

"The revenue the government raises by creating money."[304]

Interest Rates

"Interest rates, adjusted for inflation, rise and fall to balance the amount saved with the amount borrowed, which affects the allocation of scarce resources between present and future uses."[305]

K

Keynesian Economics

1.) "An economic theory of total spending in the economy and its effects on output and inflation. Keynesian economics was developed by the British economist John Maynard Keynes during the 1930s in an attempt to understand the Great Depression. Keynes advocated increased government expenditures and lower taxes to stimulate demand and pull the global economy out of the Depression."[306]

2.) "A capitalistic economy does not always employ its resources fully and that Fiscal Policy and Monetary Policy can be used to promote Full Employment."[307]

L

Law of Diminishing Returns

"When successive equal increments of a variable resource are added to the fixed resources, beyond some level of employment, the marginal product of the variable resource will decrease."[308]

Labor Force
"The total number of workers, including both the employed and unemployed."[309]

Law of Demand
"The claim that, other things equal, the quantity demanded of a good falls when the price of the good rises."[310]

Law of Supply
"The claim that, all other things equal, the quantity supplied of a good rises when the price of the good rises."[311]

Liability
"A liability of an individual or business firm is an item of value that the individual or firm owes. Many liabilities are known as debts."[312]

Liquidity
"The ease with which an asset can be converted into the economy's medium of exchange."[313]

M

M1
"The narrowly defined money supply; the currency and checkable deposits not owned by the Federal Government, Federal Reserve Banks or Depository institutions."[314]

M2
"A more broadly defined money supply; equal to M1 plus noncheckable savings deposits, small time deposits (deposits less than ($100,000,) money market deposit accounts and individual money market mutual fund balances."[315]

Macroeconomics

"The study of economy-wide phenomena, including inflation, unemployment, and economic growth."[316]

"A branch of economics dealing with the performance, structure, behavior, and decision-making of an economy as a whole, rather than individual markets."[317]

Marginal Changes

"The increase or decrease in a variable based on a small change in another variable."[318]

Market

"A market exists when buyers and sellers interact. This interaction determines market prices and thereby allocates scarce goods and services."[319]

Market Economy

"A market economy is an economy that allocates resources through the decentralized decisions of many firms and households as they interact in markets for goods and services."[320]

Market Failure

"A situation in which a market left on its own fails to allocate resources efficiently."[321]

Market Power

"The ability of a single economic actor (or small group of actors to have a substantial influence on market prices."[322]

Monetary Policy

"The setting of the money supply by policymakers in the central bank."[323]

Money

"The set of assets in an economy that people regularly use to buy goods and services from other people. Money serves three functions in our economy: medium of exchange, unit of account, and store of value."[324]

Monopoly

"A market in which the number of sellers is so small that each seller is able to influence the total supply and the price of the good or service."[325]

Monopsony

"A monopsony means there is one buyer and many sellers."[326]

Microeconomics

"The study of how households and firms make decisions and how they interact in markets."[327]

Money Multiplier

"The amount of money the banking system generates with each dollar of reserves."[328]

Money Supply

"The quantity of money available in the economy."[329]

Moral Hazard

"Insurance that lowers the cost of insured services to the insured may increase the usage of those services. This phenomenon is called 'moral hazard.' "[330]

N

Nominal GDP

"The production of goods and services valued at current prices."[331]

Nonexcludable Good

"Once a good has been created, it is impossible to prevent other people from gaining access to it (or more realistically, is extremely costly to do so)."[332]

Nonrivalrous Good

"A good is non-rivalrous if the use of the good by one individual does not limit the amount of the good available for consumption by others."[333]

Normal Good

"A good for which, other things equal, an increase in income leads to an increase in demand."[334]

O

Oligopoly

"A market in which a few firms sell either a standardized or differentiated product, into which entry is difficult, in which the firm's control over the price at which it sells its product is limited by mutual interdependence (except when there is collusion among firms,) and in which there is typically a great deal of nonprice competition."[335]

Open Market Operations

"The purchase and sale of U.S. government bonds by the Fed."[336]

Opportunity Cost

"Whatever must be given up to obtain some item."[337]

P

Phillips Curve

"A curve that shows the short-run tradeoff between inflation and unemployment."[338]

Physical Capital

"The stock of equipment and structures that are used to produce goods and services."[339]

Present Value

"The amount of money today that would be needed to produce, using prevailing interest rates, a given future amount of money."[340]

Producer Price Index

"A measure of the cost of a basket of goods and services bought by firms."[341]

Productivity

"The quantity of goods and services produced from each hour of a worker's time."[342]

Profit

"A financial benefit that is realized when the amount of revenue gained from a business activity exceeds the expenses, costs and taxes needed to sustain the activity. "[343]

Public Good

"A product that one individual can consume without reducing its availability to another individual and from which no one is excluded. Economists refer to public goods as "non-rivalrous" and "non-excludable". National defense, sewer systems, public parks and basic television and radio broadcasts could all be considered public goods."[344]

Q

Quantitative Easing

"An unconventional monetary policy in which a central bank purchases government securities or other securities from the market in order to lower interest rates and increase the money supply."[345]

Quantity Demanded

"The amount of a good that buyers are willing and able to purchase."[346]

Quantity Supplied

"The amount of a good that sellers are willing and able to sell."[347]

R

Real GDP

"The production of goods and services valued at constant prices."[348]

Recession

"A period of declining real incomes and rising unemployment."[349]

Regulatory Capture

"Regulatory capture is a theory associated with George Stigler, a Nobel laureate economist. It is the process by which regulatory agencies eventually come to be dominated by the very industries they were charged with regulating. Regulatory capture happens when a regulatory agency, formed to act in the public's interest, eventually acts in ways that benefit the industry it is supposed to be regulating, rather than the public."[350]

Rent-seeking behavior

"The pursuit through government of a transfer of income or wealth to a resource supplier, business, or consumer at someone else's or society's expense."[351]

Reserves

"Deposits that banks have received but not loaned out."[352]

Reserve Ratio

"The fraction of deposits that banks hold as reserves."[353]

Reserve Requirements

"Regulations on the minimum amount of reserves that banks must hold against deposits."[354]

Roles of Prices

"Prices send signals and provide incentives to buyers and sellers. When supply or demand changes, market prices adjust, affecting incentives."[355]

Role of Government

"There is an economic role for government in a market economy whenever the benefits of a government policy outweigh its costs. Governments often provide for national defense, address environmental concerns, define and protect property rights, and attempt to make markets more competitive. Most government policies also have direct or indirect effects on people's incomes."[356]

S

Scarcity

"Productive resources are limited. Therefore, people can not have all the goods and services they want; as a result, they must choose some things and give up others."[357]

Seigniorage

"The difference between the value of money and the cost to produce it--in other words, the economic cost of producing a currency within a given economy or country. If seigniorage is positive, then the government will make an economic profit; a negative seigniorage will result in an economic loss."[358]

Shortage

"A situation in which quantity supplied is less than quantity demanded."[359]

Solvency

"The ability of a company to meet its long-term financial obligations."[360]

Stagflation

"Inflation accompanied by stagnation in the rate of growth of output and a high unemployment rate in the economy; simultaneous increases in in both the price level and the unemployment rate."[361]

Stock

"A claim to partial ownership in a firm."[362]

Structural Unemployment

"Unemployment that results because the number of jobs available in some labor markets is insufficient to provide a job for everyone who wants one."[363]

Subprime Loan

"A type of loan that is offered at a rate above prime to individuals who do not qualify for prime rate loans. Quite often, subprime borrowers are often turned away from traditional lenders because of their low credit ratings or other factors that suggest that they have a reasonable chance of defaulting on the debt repayment"[364]

Subsidy

"Money that is paid usually by a government to keep the price of a product or service low or to help a business or organization to continue to function."[365]

Substitutes

"Two goods for which an increase in the price of one leads to an increase in the demand for the other"[366]

Supply

"Supply represents how much the market can offer. The quantity supplied refers to the amount of a certain good producers are willing to supply when receiving a certain price. The correlation between price and how much of a good or service is supplied to the market is known as the supply relationship. Price, therefore, is a reflection of supply and demand."[367]

Supply Curve

"A graph of the relationship between the price of a good and the quantity supplied."[368]

Systemically Important Financial Institution

"Financial Market Utility (FMU) as "systemically important" if the Council determines that the failure of or a disruption to the functioning of the FMU could create or increase the risk of significant liquidity or credit problems spreading among financial institutions or markets and thereby threaten the stability of the U.S. financial system."[369]

T

Tax

"A non voluntary payment of money (or goods and services) to a government by a household or a firm for which the household or firm receives no good or service directly in return and which is not a fine imposed by a court for an illegal act."[370]

Trade

"Voluntary exchange occurs only when all participating parties expect to gain. This is true for trade among individuals or organizations within a nation, and among individuals or organizations in different nations."[371]

Truth in Lending Act

"Federal Law enacted in 1968 that is designed to protect consumers who borrow; and that requires the lender to state in concise and uniform language the costs and terms of the credit (the finance charges and the annual percentage rate of interest.)"[372]

U

Unemployment Insurance
"A government program that partially protects workers' incomes when they become unemployed."[373]

Unemployment Rate
"The percentage of the labor force that is unemployed."[374]

Union
"A worker association that bargains with employers over wages and workings conditions."[375]

Utility Maximization
"Economics concept , when making a purchase decision, a consumer attempts to get the greatest value possible from expenditure of least amount of money. His or her objective is to maximize the total value derived from the available money."[376]

V

Velocity of Money
"The rate at which money changes hands."[377]

W

Wage
"The price paid for labor (for the use of or services of labor) per unit of time."[378]

Club Fed

Acknowledgements

This book would not be possible without the help of many people.

First, the great people at the Federal Reserve Bank of Minneapolis and Federal Reserve System. They are talented and dedicated in providing payment systems, banking supervision, and monetary policy.

Jenny, my wife of 28 years, provided moral support through many sleepless nights. My sons Christopher, Alexander, and Ryan gave me the confidence to continue. My mother-in-law, Judy Leahy Grimes, is a godsend.

A huge thank you to my fantastic research assistants. All of them did a fantastic job fact checking and editing the book.

Peter Fleischman did a wonderful job on the technical aspects of the project. He creatively solved the toughest problems.

T.J. Lann, aka "Econ Man," provided a good turn of phrase and gave me a deeper understanding of economics.

Megan Sacher gave me excellent guidance on the political aspects, worked hard to ensure the book had logical flow, and made sure it was easily understandable. Megan also worked to market the book effectively. `

Nick Studenski provided thoughtful economic analysis, vetted the book for logical and grammatical errors, and was never afraid to ask "why?"

I would like to thank Art Rolnick, Ed Prescott, Sam Goaley, Wade Vitalis, Fred Martin, Matt Kaul and Kris Sommerville for their insightful interviews. Dave Dahl is a great mentor.

I would like to thank all of my editors for their help: , Cheryl Weiberg, Richard Sine, Cindy Tregilgas, Jewel Pickert, Matthew Kaul, Daniel Dickinson, and Glen Swenson.

Club Fed

Thanks to all my brothers and sisters: Monica, Ted, Todd, Colleen, Tom, Thad, Terry, Missy, Timmy, and Molly. My inlaws Amy, Nora, and Jessica. My Outlaws: Dave, Diane, Lisa, Mark, Tippy, Cara, Greg, Chuck, and Louise.

Thanks to everyone who supported the project on Kickstarter.

Endnotes

Endnotes:

[1] Davies, P. (2008, September 1). The Rise and Fall of Nicholas Biddle. Retrieved July 8, 2015, from https://www.minneapolisfed.org/publications/the-region/the-rise-and-fall-of-nicholas-biddle

[2] A History of Central Banking in the United States. (n.d.). Retrieved July 27, 2015, from https://www.minneapolisfed.org/community/student-resources/central-bank-history/history-of-central-banking

[3] Rolnick, A. (2015, July 13). Personal interview.

[4] Functions of Money. (n.d.). Retrieved July 9, 2015, from http://staffwww.fullcoll.edu/fchan/macro/4functions_of_money.htm

[5] Obscura, A. (n.d.). Cash, Card, or Car-Sized Stone: The Island Where Giant Stones Are Currency. Retrieved July 27, 2015, from http://www.slate.com/blogs/atlas_obscura/2013/10/15/cash_card_or_car_sized_stone_payment_options_on_the_island_of_yap.html

[6] 10.26.96, P. (n.d.). The History of Money. Retrieved July 27, 2015, from http://www.pbs.org/wgbh/nova/ancient/history-money.html

[7] 10.26.96, P. (n.d.). The History of Money. Retrieved July 27, 2015, from http://www.pbs.org/wgbh/nova/ancient/history-money.html

[8] 10.26.96, P. (n.d.). The History of Money. Retrieved July 27, 2015, from http://www.pbs.org/wgbh/nova/ancient/history-money.html

[9] History Of Salt. (n.d.). Retrieved July 27, 2015, from http://www.saltworks.us/salt_info/si_HistoryOfSalt.asp#historyecon

[10] Cocoa Bean Currency. (n.d.). Retrieved July 27, 2015, from http://encyclopedia-of-money.blogspot.com/2010/01/cocoa-bean-currency.html

[11] Who Accepts Bitcoins As Payment? List of Companies. (2014, February 19). Retrieved July 27, 2015, from http://www.bitcoinvalues.net/who-accepts-bitcoins-payment-companies-stores-take-bitcoins.html

[12] Frequently Asked Questions. (n.d.). Retrieved July 27, 2015, from https://bitcoin.org/en/faq

[13] The United States Mint · About Us. (n.d.). Retrieved July 27, 2015, from http://www.usmint.gov/about_the_mint/mint_facilities/?action=pa_facilities

[14] U.S. Mint History Since 1792. (n.d.). Retrieved August 3, 2015, from http://us-mint.info/index.html

[15] El Salvador learns to love the greenback. (2002, September 28). Retrieved July 27, 2015, from http://www.economist.com/node/1357779

[16] Cipheritis. (1923, December 17). Retrieved July 27, 2015, from http://content.time.com/time/magazine/article/0,9171,717208,00.html

[17] Piggy bank; Argentina's economy. (2012, March 31). The Economist.

[18] XE Currency Charts. (n.d.). Retrieved July 14, 2015, from http://www.xe.com/currencycharts/?from=USD&to=ARS&view=5Y

[19] Board Members. (n.d.). Retrieved July 27, 2015, from http://www.federalreserve.gov/aboutthefed/bios/board/default.htm

[20] FRB: Mission, Values, and Goals of the Board of Governors: Government Performance and Results Act 2011. (n.d.). Retrieved July 27, 2015, from http://www.federalreserve.gov/publications/gpra/2011-mission-values-and-goals-of-the-board-of-governors.htm#subsection-144-21C3B972

[21] Rolnick, A. (2015, July 13). Personal interview.

[22] *It's a Wonderful Life* [Motion picture]. (1946). Goodtimes Home Video

[23] Sigurjonsson, F. (n.d.). A Better Monetary System for Iceland. Retrieved July 8, 2015, from http://eng.forsaetisraduneyti.is/media/Skyrslur/monetary-reform.pdf

[24] Panic of 1907. (n.d.). Retrieved August 3, 2015, from https://www.bostonfed.org/about/pubs/panicof1.pdf

[25] The 1907 Crisis in Historical Perspective. (n.d.). Retrieved July 8, 2015, from http://www.fas.harvard.edu/~histecon/crisis-next/1907/index.html

[26] Rolnick, A. (2015, July 13). Personal interview.

[27] Federal Reserve Act. (n.d.). Retrieved July 20, 2015.

[28] FRB: Federal Reserve Districts and Banks. (n.d.). Retrieved July 8, 2015, from http://www.federalreserve.gov/otherfrb.htm

[29] Current FAQs Informing the public about the Federal Reserve. (n.d.). Retrieved July 27, 2015, from http://www.federalreserve.gov/faqs/about_12594.htm

[30] Rolnick, A. (2015, July 13). Personal interview.

[31] Dodd-Frank Act. (n.d.). Retrieved July 30, 2015, from http://www.cftc.gov/lawregulation/doddfrankact/index.htm

[32] Financial Stability Oversight Council. (n.d.). Retrieved July 20, 2015, from http://www.treasury.gov/initiatives/fsoc/designations/Pages/default.aspx

[33] Federal Open Market Committee. (n.d.). Retrieved July 27, 2015, from http://www.federalreserve.gov/monetarypolicy/fomc.htm

[34] The Federal Reserve's Dual Mandate. (n.d.). Retrieved July 27, 2015, from https://www.chicagofed.org/publications/speeches/our-dual-mandate-background

[35] Prescott, E. (2015, July 7). Personal interview.

Endnotes

---

[36] Current Report: 2014. (n.d.). Retrieved July 27, 2015, from
http://www.federalreserve.gov/publications/annual-report/

[37] FRB: How much U.S. currency is in circulation? (n.d.). Retrieved July 29, 2015, from
http://www.federalreserve.gov/faqs/currency_12773.htm

[38] Credit and Liquidity Programs and the Balance Sheet. (n.d.). Retrieved July 8, 2015, from
http://www.federalreserve.gov/monetarypolicy/bst_fedfinancials.htm

[39] Federal Deposit Insurance Corporation. (n.d.). Retrieved July 10, 2015, from
https://www.fdic.gov/regulations/laws/rules/8000-2200.html

[40] Check Services. (n.d.). Retrieved July 10, 2015, from
http://www.federalreserve.gov/paymentsystems/check_about.htm

[41] Check Services. (n.d.). Retrieved July 10, 2015, from
http://www.federalreserve.gov/paymentsystems/check_about.htm

[42] Sarmiento, M. (2009). Central Bank Economic Research: Output, Demand, Productivity, and Relevance. Borradores de Economía, 576, p. 1-7

[43] Rolnick, A. (2015, July 13). Personal interview.

[44] Dahl, D. (2015, July 6).Telephone interview.

[45] Rolnick, A. Résumé. (n.d.) Retrieved July 9, 2015 from
http://www.hhh.umn.edu/people/arolnick/pdf/Rolnickresume.pdf

[46] Community Reinvestment Act. (n.d.). Retrieved July 16, 2015, from
http://www.federalreserve.gov/communitydev/cra_about.htm

[47] Sabia, J., Pitts, M., & Argys, L. (n.d.). Do Minimum Wages Really Increase Youth Drinking and Drunk Driving? Retrieved July 15, 2015.

[48] Prescott, E. (2015, July 7). Personal interview.

[49] Rolnick, A. (2015, July 13). Personal interview.

[50] Kocherlakota, N. (2015). Persistent Poverty on Indian Reservations: New Perspectives and Responses. The Region, 29(2), 5-6.

[51] Geiger, K. (2015, February 1). Rauner faces immediate test as Illinois runs out of daycare money. Retrieved July 9, 2015.

[52] An Update on State Budget Cuts. (n.d.). Retrieved July 27, 2015, from
http://www.cbpp.org/research/an-update-on-state-budget-cuts

[53] Dahl, D. (2015, July 6). Telephone interview.

[54] Hoenig, T. (n.d.). Twelve Banks: The Strength of The Federal Reserve. Retrieved July 20, 2015, from http://www.frbsf.org/education/publications/doctor-econ/2001/may/0501.pdf

---

[55] The biggest mass layoffs of the past two decades. (n.d.). Retrieved August 3, 2015, from http://www.washingtonpost.com/news/on-leadership/wp/2015/01/28/the-biggest-mass-layoffs-of-the-past-two-decades/

[56] Mills, D. (1996, July 15) The Decline and Rise of IBM. Retrieved July 9, 2015 from http://sloanreview.mit.edu/article/the-decline-and-rise-of-ibm/

[57] Clark, D. (2014, August 24) John Akers, IBM Former Chief, Dies at 79. Retrieved July 9, 2015 from http://www.wsj.com/articles/john-akers-ibm-former-chief-dies-at-79-1408920798

[58] Pitts, G. (2014, April 24) Turnaround ace: Inside the Hunter Harrison era at CP Railway. Retrieved July 9, 2015 from http://www.theglobeandmail.com/report-on-business/rob-magazine/hunter-harrison-cp-report-on-business-magazine/article18190120/

[59] The Canadian Press. (2012, December 4) CP Rail Cutting 4,500 Jobs: Shares Spike On Announcement. Retrieved July 9, 2015 from http://www.huffingtonpost.ca/2012/12/04/cp-rail-cutting-4500-jobs_n_2241063.html

[60] Nelson, T; Moylan, M. (2015, March 10) A 'difficult day' as Target lays off 1,700. Retrieved July 9, 2015 from http://www.mprnews.org/story/2015/03/10/target-layoffs

[61] Hammerand, J. (2015, June 15). Target sells pharmacies to CVS for $1.9B; Could cut HQ jobs. Retrieved July 29, 2015, from http://www.bizjournals.com/twincities/morning_roundup/2015/06/target-sells-pharmacies-to-cvs-for-1-9b-could-cut.html

[62] Wahba, P. (2015, March 1) Target has a new CEO: will he re-energize the retailer? Retrieved July 9, 2015 from http://fortune.com/target-new-ceo/

[63] Press Release. (n.d.). Retrieved July 23, 2015 http://www.federalreserve.gov/newsevents/press/other/20091125a.htm

[64] Press Release. (n.d.). Retrieved July 23, 2015, from http://www.federalreserve.gov/newsevents/press/other/20091125a.htm

[65] William C. Dudley - Federal Reserve Bank of New York. (n.d.). Retrieved July 8, 2015, from http://www.newyorkfed.org/aboutthefed/orgchart/dudley.html

[66] Timothy F. Geithner. (n.d.). Retrieved July 8, 2015, from http://www.warburgpincus.com/people/ViewEmployee,employeeid,449.aspx

[67] E. Gerald Corrigan. (1999). In *Chapter Summary*. University of North Texas.

[68] Henry M. Paulson, Jr. (2015, March 18). Retrieved July 8, 2015, from http://www.paulsoninstitute.org/about/about-our-people/

[69] Acemoglu, D., & Johnson, S. (2012, March 29). Who Captured the Fed? Retrieved July 10, 2015.

[70] Current FAQs Informing the public about the Federal Reserve. (n.d.). Retrieved July 23, 2015, from http://www.federalreserve.gov/faqs/about_12594.htm

[71] Gary H. Stern. (2009, February). *Prospects for Macro- and Financial Policy.* Speech presented at Capital City Partnership Annual Meeting, St. Paul, MN.

Endnotes

[72] Prescott, E. (2015, July 7). Personal interview.

[73] Geithner, T. F. (2015). Stress Test: Reflections on Financial Crises. New York: Broadway Books.

[74] Rolnick, A. (2015, July 13). Personal interview.

[75] Katz, I., & Kearns, J. (n.d.). Dudley Defends N.Y. Fed as Senators See Coziness With Banks. Retrieved July 8, 2015, from http://www.bloomberg.com/news/articles/2014-11-21/dudley-defends-new-york-fed-supervision-in-heated-senate-hearing

[76] Rolnick, A (2015, July 13). Personal interview.

[77] What We Do. (n.d.). Retrieved July 9, 2015, from http://www.ny.frb.org/aboutthefed/whatwedo.html

[78] Regulatory Capture 101. (2014, October 6). Retrieved July 9, 2015, from http://www.wsj.com/articles/regulatory-capture-101-1412544509

[79] Cieslak, A., Morse, A., & Vissing-Jorgensen, A. (2014, April 23). Stock Returns over the FOMC Cycle. Retrieved July 8, 2015, from http://faculty.haas.berkeley.edu/vissing/CieslakMorseVissing.pdf

[80] Prescott, E. (2015, July 7). Personal interview.

[81] Dodd-Frank Act Stress Test (Company-Run). (n.d.). Retrieved July 10, 2015, from http://www.occ.gov/tools-forms/forms/bank-operations/stress-test-reporting.html

[82] Stress Tests and Capital Planning. (n.d.). Retrieved July 10, 2015, from http://www.federalreserve.gov/bankinforeg/stress-tests-capital-planning.htm

[83] 5 biggest banks now own almost half the industry. (2015, April 15). Retrieved July 9, 2015, from http://www.cnbc.com/2015/04/15/5-biggest-banks-now-own-almost-half-the-industry.html

[84] Each depositor insured to at least $250,000 per insured bank. (n.d.). Retrieved July 9, 2015, from https://www2.fdic.gov/hsob/HSOBRpt.asp

[85] Jones, K., & Critchfield, T. (2005). Consolidation in the U.S. Banking Industry: Is the "Long, Strange Trip" About to End? *Handbook of Financial Intermediation and Banking, 17*(4), 309-346. Retrieved July 9, 2015, from https://www.fdic.gov/bank/analytical/banking/2006jan/article2/article2.pdf

[86] I noticed that banks have dramatically increased their excess reserve holdings. Is this buildup of reserves related to monetary policy? (n.d.). Retrieved July 9, 2015, from http://www.frbsf.org/education/publications/doctor-econ/2010/march/banks-excess-reserves-monetary-policy

[87] Laeven, L., Ratnovski, L., & Tong, H. (2014, May 1). Bank Size and Systematic Risk. Retrieved July 9, 2015, from http://www.imf.org/external/pubs/ft/sdn/2014/sdn1404.pdf

[88] Wheelock, D., & Wilson, P. (2011, May 1). Do Large Banks have Lower Costs? New Estimates of Returns to Scale for U.S. Banks. Retrieved July 9, 2015, from http://www.clemson.edu/economics/faculty/wilson/Papers/ww-cost.pdf

[89] Corus Bank Audit Report. (n.d.). Retrieved July 13, 2015, from http://www.treasury.gov/about/organizational-structure/ig/Agency Documents/Corus MLR Final with s.pdf

[90] Written Agreement By Corus Bankshares and The Federal Reserve. (n.d.). Retrieved July 10, 2015, from http://www.federalreserve.gov/newsevents/press/enforcement/enf20090219d1.pdf

[91] Corus Bankshares, Inc. Schedule 13D dated June 1, 2009. (n.d.) Retrieved July 15, 2015, from http://www.sec.gov/Archives/edgar/data/51939/000114420409030329/v151246_sc-13d.htm

[92] Corus Bankshares, Inc. Schedule 13D dated June 9,2009 (n.d.) Retrieved July 15, 2015 from http://www.sec.gov/Archives/edgar/data/51939/000114420409031676/v151923_scl3d-a.htm

[93] Corus Bank Audit Report. (n.d.). Retrieved July 13, 2015, from http://www.treasury.gov/about/organizational-structure/ig/Agency Documents/Corus MLR Final with s.pdf

[94] Corus Bankshares, Inc. Form 10-K 2008 Annual Report. (n.d.). Retrieved July 14, 2015, from https://www.sec.gov/Archives/edgar/data/51939/000136231009004935/c83241e10vk.htm

[95] Each depositor insured to at least $250,000 per insured bank. (n.d.). Retrieved July 30, 2015, from https://www.fdic.gov/bank/individual/failed/midwestil.html

[96] Olde Cypress Bank Review. (n.d.). Retrieved July 13, 2015, from http://www.treasury.gov/about/organizational-structure/ig/Documents/OIG10052 (Olde Cypress Limited Review).pdf

[97] SAFETY AND SOUNDNESS: Failed Bank Review of Turnberry Bank. (2010, September 29). Retrieved July 30, 2015.

[98] Western Springs Review. (n.d.). Retrieved July 13, 2015, from http://www.treasury.gov/about/organizational-structure/ig/Documents/9 8 11 Western - Limited Assessment Final Electronic (2).pdf

[99] United Americas Bank Review. (n.d.). Retrieved July 13, 2015, from http://www.treasury.gov/about/organizational-structure/ig/Documents/Limited Review Memo - United Americas Bank.pdf

[100] Carolina Federal Savings Bank Review. (n.d.). Retrieved July 13, 2015, from http://www.treasury.gov/about/organizational-structure/ig/Audit Reports and Testimonies/OIG-12-067.pdf

[101] Rolnick, A. (2015, July 13). Personal interview.

[102] Katz, I., & Boesler, M. (2015, April 20). Fed Weighs Steps to Prevent 'Regulatory Capture' by Banks. Retrieved July 9, 2015, from http://www.bloomberg.com/news/articles/2015-04-20/fed-said-to-weigh-steps-to-prevent-regulatory-capture-by-banks

[103] Rolnick, A (2015, July 12). Personal interview.

[104] Federal Reserve Act. (n.d.). Retrieved July 9, 2015, from http://www.federalreserve.gov/aboutthefed/section7.htm

Endnotes

[105] Opportunities Exist to Broaden Director Recruitment Efforts and Increase Transparency. (2011, October 1). Retrieved July 9, 2015, from http://www.gao.gov/assets/590/585807.pdf

[106] Fed Conference Call Helps Banks Navigate CRE Loan Workouts. (n.d.). Retrieved July 9, 2015

[107] Fed Conference Call Helps Banks Navigate CRE Loan Workouts. (n.d.). Retrieved July 20, 2015.

[108] Vitalis, W. (2015, July 4). Email Interview.

[109] Financial Accounts of the United States First Quarter 2015. (n.d.). Retrieved July 17, 2015.

[110] FRB: Survey of Consumer Finances 2013. (n.d.). Retrieved July 17, 2015.

[111] Nakajima, M. (2015). The Redistributive Consequences of Monetary Policy. *Business Review*. Retrieved July 16, 2015

[112] Kaul, M. (2015, July 14). Personal interview.

[113] Matthews, S. (2015, April 15). Bullard Says Zero Policy Rate Risks Asset-Price Bubbles. Retrieved July 20, 2015.

[114] Eisen, B. (2014, June 26). Kevin Warsh: Fed policy is 'reverse Robin Hood' Retrieved July 16, 2015, from http://www.marketwatch.com/story/kevin-warsh-fed-policy-is-reverse-robin-hood-2014-06-26

[115] Buttonwood. (2014, November 27). Send in the helicopters? Retrieved July 20, 2015, from http://www.economist.com/blogs/buttonwood/2014/11/reviving-economy

[116] Prescott, E. (2015, July 7). Personal interview.

[117] Robb, G.(2015, July 7) IMF warns Fed on risks of hiking too soon. Retrieved July 9, 2015

[118] Rolnick, A. (2015, July 13). Personal interview.

[119] Martin, F (2015, July 16). Personal interview.

[120] Paulson, H. (2015). Dealing with China: An insider unmasks the new economic superpower.

[121] Hepburn, A., & Hepburn, E. (1967). A history of currency in the United States (Rev. ed.). New York: A.M. Kelley.

[122] Michener, R. (n.d.). Money in the American Colonies. Retrieved July 8, 2015, from http://eh.net/encyclopedia/money-in-the-american-colonies/

[123] Hamilton's Political Vision and the Federalist Papers - Boundless Open Textbook. (n.d.). Retrieved July 8, 2015, from https://www.boundless.com/u-s-history/textbooks/boundless-u-s-history-textbook/the-federalist-era-1789-1801-10/hamilton-s-economic-policy-87/hamilton-s-political-vision-and-the-federalist-papers-485-7919/

224

[124] Hamilton vs. Jefferson. (n.d.). Retrieved July 8, 2015, from http://www.let.rug.nl/usa/outlines/history-1994/the-formation-of-a-national-government/hamilton-vs-jefferson.php

[125] Founders Online: To George Washington from Thomas Jefferson, 15 February 1791. (n.d.). Retrieved May 29, 2015, from http://founders.archives.gov/documents/Washington/05-07-02-0207

[126] McCulloch v. Maryland. (n.d.). Retrieved July 8, 2015, from https://www.law.cornell.edu/supremecourt/text/17/316

[127] Osborn v. Bank of the United States. (n.d.). Retrieved July 8, 2015, from http://www.oyez.org/cases/1792-1850/1824/1824_2

[128] Second Bank of the United States (1816-1836). (n.d.). Retrieved July 8, 2015, from http://www.let.rug.nl/usa/essays/general/a-brief-history-of-central-banking/second-bank-of-the-united-states-(1816-1836).php

[129] Bank War. (n.d.). Retrieved July 8, 2015, from http://www.history.com/topics/bank-war

[130] Wile, R. (2013, February 11). The Crazy Story Of The Time When Almost Anyone In America Could Issue Their Own Currency. Retrieved July 8, 2015, from http://www.businessinsider.com/history-of-the-free-bank-era-2013-2#the-circular-sparks-a-bank-run-on-specie-instant-devaluation-and-recession-5

[131] Congress and the Constitution: the Legal Tender Act of 1862 Pai, Ajit V.Oregon Law Review, Summer, 1998, Vol.77(2), p.535-599

[132] National Banking Acts of 1863 and 1864. (n.d.). Retrieved July 23, 2015.

[133] Reinhart, C., & Rogoff, K. (2009). This time is different: Eight centuries of financial folly (pp. 6-7). Princeton: Princeton University Press.

[134] Leab, D. (2014). Encyclopedia of American recessions and depressions. Santa Barbara: ABC-CLIO.

[135] Bubbles, Panics & Crashes – Historical Collections – Harvard Business School. (n.d.). Retrieved July 23, 2015.

[136] Leab, D. (2014). Encyclopedia of American recessions and depressions. Santa Barbara: ABC-CLIO.

[137] The Panic of 1873. (n.d.). Retrieved July 8, 2015, from http://www.pbs.org/wgbh/americanexperience/features/general-article/grant-panic/

[138] Skrabec, Q. (2014). The 100 most important American financial crises: An encyclopedia of the lowest points in American economic history. Greenwood.

[139] *Encyclopedia of American Recessions and Depressions* Daniel J. Leab 2014

[140] 1896: Economic Depression. (n.d.). Retrieved July 23, 2015, from http://projects.vassar.edu/1896/depression.html

Endnotes

[141] United States Circuit Courts of Appeals reports. (1913). Retrieved from https://books.google.com/books?id=N3VNAQAAIAAJ

[142] The 1907 Crisis in Historical Perspective. (n.d.). Retrieved July 8, 2015, from http://www.fas.harvard.edu/~histecon/crisis-next/1907/index.html

[143] The Federal Reserve System: Purposes and Functions. (n.d.). Retrieved July 22, 2015, from http://www.federalreserve.gov/pf/pdf/pf_complete.pdf

[144] History of the Federal Reserve. (n.d.). Retrieved July 8, 2015, from https://www.federalreserveeducation.org/about-the-fed/history

[145] The Great Depression. (n.d.). Retrieved July 8, 2015, from http://www.pbs.org/wgbh/americanexperience/features/general-article/dustbowl-great-depression/

[146] Ghizoni, S. (n.d.). Establishment of the Bretton Woods System. Retrieved July 9, 2015, from http://www.federalreservehistory.org/Events/DetailView/28

[147] Walstad, W., & Bingham, R. (1993). Glossary. In Study guide to accompany McConnell and Brue twelfth edition economics (p. 480). New York: McGraw-Hill.

[148] Yergin, D., & Stanislaw, J. (n.d.). Nixon, Price Controls, and the Gold Standard. Retrieved July 20, 2015.

[149] Savings and Loan Crisis. (2009, January 28). Retrieved July 8, 2015, from http://www.investopedia.com/terms/s/sl-crisis.asp#ixzz3cfpLSrNm

[150] Federal Reserve Banks announce changes to increase check service efficiency. (2007, June 26). Retrieved July 8, 2015, from http://www.federalreserve.gov/newsevents/press/other/20070626a.htm

[151] Check Processing - Fedpoints - Federal Reserve Bank of New York. (n.d.). Retrieved July 23, 2015.

[152] Financial Crisis Timeline. (n.d.). Retrieved July 8, 2015, from https://www.stlouisfed.org/financial-crisis/full-timeline

[153] Dodd-Frank Financial Regulatory Reform Bill Definition | Investopedia. (2010, July 21). Retrieved July 23, 2015.

[154] Financial Statements as of and for the Years Ended December 31, 2014 and 2013 and Independent Auditors' Report. (n.d.). Retrieved July 17, 2015, from http://www.federalreserve.gov/monetarypolicy/files/BSTAtlantafinstmt2014.pdf

[155] FRB: 2015 Reserve Bank Budgets. (n.d.). Retrieved July 23, 2015, from http://www.federalreserve.gov/foia/2015rb_budgets.htm#tbb

[156] Central Bank Economic Research: Output, Demand, Productivity, and Relevance. (n.d.). Retrieved July 22, 2015.

[157] 101st Annual Report. (n.d.). Retrieved July 17, 2015, from http://www.federalreserve.gov/publications/annual-report/files/2014-annual-report.pdf

[158] Sabia, J., Pitts, M., & Argys, L. (2014, November 1). Do Minimum Wages Really Increase Youth Drinking and Drunk Driving? Retrieved July 17, 2015, from https://www.frbatlanta.org/research/publications/wp/2014/14_20.aspx

[159] Center for Human Capital Studies. (n.d.). Retrieved July 17, 2015, from https://www.frbatlanta.org/chcs.aspx

[160] Carpenter, A. (2013, September 1). Social Ties, Space, and Resilience: Literature Review of Community Resilience to Disasters and Constituent Social and Built

[161] Broke: Financial Lessons from Athletes. (2015, June 10). Retrieved July 17, 2015, from https://www.frbatlanta.org/forms/education/workshops-events/2015/0610-bhm

[162] Financial Statements as of and for the Years Ended December 31, 2014 and 2013 and Independent Auditors' Report. (n.d.). Retrieved July 17, 2015, from http://www.federalreserve.gov/monetarypolicy/files/BSTBostonfinstmt2014.pdf

[163] FRB: 2015 Reserve Bank Budgets. (n.d.). Retrieved July 23, 2015, from http://www.federalreserve.gov/foia/2015rb_budgets.htm#tbb

[164] Central Bank Economic Research: Output, Demand, Productivity, and Relevance. (n.d.). Retrieved July 22, 2015.

[165] 101st Annual Report. (n.d.). Retrieved July 17, 2015, from http://www.federalreserve.gov/publications/annual-report/files/2014-annual-report.pdf

[166] Watson, T. (2013). Enforcement and Immigrant Location Choice. Retrieved July 17, 2015, from http://www.bostonfed.org/economic/wp/wp2013/wp1310.htm

[167] Shy, O. (2013). Window Shopping. Retrieved July 17, 2015, from http://www.bostonfed.org/economic/wp/wp2013/wp1304.htm

[168] Community Development. (n.d.). Retrieved July 17, 2015, from http://www.bostonfed.org/commdev/index.htm

[169] Financial Statements as of and for the Years Ended December 31, 2014 and 2013 and Independent Auditors' Report. (n.d.). Retrieved July 17, 2015, from http://www.federalreserve.gov/monetarypolicy/files/BSTChicagofinstmt2014.pdf

[170] FRB: 2015 Reserve Bank Budgets. (n.d.). Retrieved July 23, 2015, from http://www.federalreserve.gov/foia/2015rb_budgets.htm#tbb

[171] Central Bank Economic Research: Output, Demand, Productivity, and Relevance. (n.d.). Retrieved July 22, 2015.

[172] 101st Annual Report. (n.d.). Retrieved July 17, 2015, from http://www.federalreserve.gov/publications/annual-report/files/2014-annual-report.pdf

[173] Saving Europe?: The Unpleasant Arithmetic of Fiscal Austerity in Integrated Economies - Federal Reserve Bank of Chicago. (n.d.). Retrieved July 20, 2015.

[174] Early Life Environment and Racial Inequality in Education and Earnings in the United States - Federal Reserve Bank of Chicago. (n.d.). Retrieved July 20, 2015.

[175] Financial Statements as of and for the Years Ended December 31, 2014 and 2013 and Independent Auditors' Report. (n.d.). Retrieved July 17, 2015, from http://www.federalreserve.gov/monetarypolicy/files/BSTClevelandsfinstmt2014.pdf

Endnotes

176 FRB: 2015 Reserve Bank Budgets. (n.d.). Retrieved July 23, 2015, from http://www.federalreserve.gov/foia/2015rb_budgets.htm#tbb

177 Central Bank Economic Research: Output, Demand, Productivity, and Relevance. (n.d.). Retrieved July 22, 2015

178 101st Annual Report. (n.d.). Retrieved July 17, 2015, from http://www.federalreserve.gov/publications/annual-report/files/2014-annual-report.pdf

179 Hinrichs, P. (2014, December 1). What Kind of Teachers Are Schools Looking For?

180 Baum-Snow, N., & Hartley, D. (n.d.). Demographic Changes in and near US Downtowns. Retrieved July 30, 2015, from https://www.clevelandfed.org/en/Newsroom and Events/Publications/Economic Trends/2015/et 20150605 demographic changes in and near us downtowns.aspx

181 Financial Statements as of and for the Years Ended December 31, 2014 and 2013 and Independent Auditors' Report. (n.d.). Retrieved July 17, 2015, from http://www.federalreserve.gov/monetarypolicy/files/BSTDallasfinstmt2014.pdf

182 FRB: 2015 Reserve Bank Budgets. (n.d.). Retrieved July 23, 2015, from http://www.federalreserve.gov/foia/2015rb_budgets.htm#tbb

183 Central Bank Economic Research: Output, Demand, Productivity, and Relevance. (n.d.). Retrieved July 22, 2015.

184 101st Annual Report. (n.d.). Retrieved July 17, 2015, from http://www.federalreserve.gov/publications/annual-report/files/2014-annual-report.pdf

185 Tourism and Recreation a Bright Spot in the Big Bend Region. (n.d.). Retrieved July 20, 2015.

186 Financial Statements as of and for the Years Ended December 31, 2014 and 2013 and Independent Auditors' Report. (n.d.). Retrieved July 17, 2015, from http://www.federalreserve.gov/monetarypolicy/files/BSTKansasCityfinstmt2014.pdf

187 FRB: 2015 Reserve Bank Budgets. (n.d.). Retrieved July 23, 2015, from http://www.federalreserve.gov/foia/2015rb_budgets.htm#tbb

188 Central Bank Economic Research: Output, Demand, Productivity, and Relevance. (n.d.). Retrieved July 22, 2015.

189 101st Annual Report. (n.d.). Retrieved July 17, 2015, from http://www.federalreserve.gov/publications/annual-report/files/2014-annual-report.pdf

190 Student Loans Overview and Issues. (n.d.). Retrieved July 20, 2015.

191 Nonprofit Housing Investment and Local Area Home Values. (n.d.). Retrieved July 20, 2015.

192 Financial Statements as of and for the Years Ended December 31, 2014 and 2013 and Independent Auditors' Report. (n.d.). Retrieved July 17, 2015, from http://www.federalreserve.gov/monetarypolicy/files/BSTMinneapolisfinstmt2014.pdf

193 FRB: 2015 Reserve Bank Budgets. (n.d.). Retrieved July 23, 2015, from http://www.federalreserve.gov/foia/2015rb_budgets.htm#tbb

194 Central Bank Economic Research: Output, Demand, Productivity, and Relevance. (n.d.). Retrieved July 22, 2015.

195 101st Annual Report. (n.d.). Retrieved July 17, 2015, from http://www.federalreserve.gov/publications/annual-report/files/2014-annual-report.pdf

196 Organize it, and they will come? | Federal Reserve Bank of Minneapolis. (n.d.). Retrieved July 20, 2015.

197 Taxing Wealth | Federal Reserve Bank of Minneapolis. (n.d.). Retrieved July 20, 2015.

198 How Rich Will China Become? | Federal Reserve Bank of Minneapolis. (n.d.). Retrieved July 20, 2015.

199 Indian Country. (n.d.). Retrieved July 20, 2015, from https://minneapolisfed.org/community/indian-country

200 Financial Statements as of and for the Years Ended December 31, 2014 and 2013 and Independent Auditors' Report. (n.d.). Retrieved July 17, 2015, from http://www.federalreserve.gov/monetarypolicy/files/BSTNewYorkfinstmt2014.pdf ?

201 FRB: 2015 Reserve Bank Budgets. (n.d.). Retrieved July 23, 2015, from http://www.federalreserve.gov/foia/2015rb_budgets.htm#tbb

202 Central Bank Economic Research: Output, Demand, Productivity, and Relevance. (n.d.). Retrieved July 22, 2015.

203 101st Annual Report. (n.d.). Retrieved July 17, 2015, from http://www.federalreserve.gov/publications/annual-report/files/2014-annual-report.pdf

204 Are Recent College Graduates Finding Good Jobs. (n.d.). Retrieved July 20, 2015.

205 The Causes and Consequences of Puerto Rico's Declining Population - Federal Reserve Bank of New York. (n.d.). Retrieved July 20, 2015.

206 Do the Benefits of College Still Outweigh the Costs? (n.d.). Retrieved July 20, 2015.

207 Financial Statements as of and for the Years Ended December 31, 2014 and 2013 and Independent Auditors' Report. (n.d.). Retrieved July 17, 2015, from http://www.federalreserve.gov/monetarypolicy/files/BSTPhiladelphiafinstmt2014.pdf

208 FRB: 2015 Reserve Bank Budgets. (n.d.). Retrieved July 23, 2015, from http://www.federalreserve.gov/foia/2015rb_budgets.htm#tbb

209 Central Bank Economic Research: Output, Demand, Productivity, and Relevance. (n.d.). Retrieved July 22, 2015.

210 101st Annual Report. (n.d.). Retrieved July 17, 2015, from http://www.federalreserve.gov/publications/annual-report/files/2014-annual-report.pdf

211 History and the Sizes of Cities. (n.d.). Retrieved July 20, 2015.

212 Weather-Adjusting Employment Data. (n.d.). Retrieved July 20, 2015.

213 Identity Theft as a Teachable Moment. (n.d.). Retrieved July 20, 2015.

214 Azzimonti, M. (n.d.). Partisan Conflict. Retrieved July 20, 2015.

Endnotes

215 Financial Statements as of and for the Years Ended December 31, 2014 and 2013 and Independent Auditors' Report. (n.d.). Retrieved July 17, 2015, from http://www.federalreserve.gov/monetarypolicy/files/BSTRichmondfinstmt2014.pdf

216 FRB: 2015 Reserve Bank Budgets. (n.d.). Retrieved July 23, 2015, from http://www.federalreserve.gov/foia/2015rb_budgets.htm#tbb

217 Central Bank Economic Research: Output, Demand, Productivity, and Relevance. (n.d.). Retrieved July 22, 2015.

218 101st Annual Report. (n.d.). Retrieved July 17, 2015, from http://www.federalreserve.gov/publications/annual-report/files/2014-annual-report.pdf

219 Learning and Life Cycle Patterns of Occupational Transitions. (n.d.). Retrieved July 20, 2015.

220 Financial Statements as of and for the Years Ended December 31, 2014 and 2013 and Independent Auditors' Report. (n.d.). Retrieved July 17, 2015, from http://www.federalreserve.gov/monetarypolicy/files/BSTSanFranciscofinstmt2014.pdf

221 FRB: 2015 Reserve Bank Budgets. (n.d.). Retrieved July 23, 2015, from http://www.federalreserve.gov/foia/2015rb_budgets.htm#tbb

222 Central Bank Economic Research: Output, Demand, Productivity, and Relevance. (n.d.). Retrieved July 22, 2015.

223 101st Annual Report. (n.d.). Retrieved July 17, 2015, from http://www.federalreserve.gov/publications/annual-report/files/2014-annual-report.pdf

224 Does Medicare Part D Save Lives? (n.d.). Retrieved July 20, 2015.

225 The Changing Role of Disabled Children Benefits. (n.d.). Retrieved July 20, 2015.

226 The Lifelong Effects of Early Childhood Poverty. (n.d.). Retrieved July 20, 2015.

227 Financial Statements as of and for the Years Ended December 31, 2014 and 2013 and Independent Auditors' Report. (n.d.). Retrieved July 17, 2015, from http://www.federalreserve.gov/monetarypolicy/files/BSTSt.Louisfinstmt2014.pdf

228 FRB: 2015 Reserve Bank Budgets. (n.d.). Retrieved July 23, 2015, from http://www.federalreserve.gov/foia/2015rb_budgets.htm#tbb

229 Central Bank Economic Research: Output, Demand, Productivity, and Relevance. (n.d.). Retrieved July 22, 2015.

230 101st Annual Report. (n.d.). Retrieved July 17, 2015, from http://www.federalreserve.gov/publications/annual-report/files/2014-annual-report.pdf

231 Fertility Shocks and Equilibrium Marriage-Rate Dynamics. (n.d.). Retrieved July 20, 2015.

232 Schools and Stimulus. (n.d.). Retrieved July 20, 2015.

233 Center for Household Financial Stability. (n.d.). Retrieved July 20, 2015.

234 101st Annual Report. (n.d.). Retrieved July 17, 2015, from http://www.federalreserve.gov/publications/annual-report/files/2014-annual-report.pdf

[235] FRB: Annual Report 2013 - Federal Reserve System Budgets. (n.d.). Retrieved July 23, 2015, from http://www.federalreserve.gov/publications/annual-report/2013-federal-reserve-system-budgets.htm

[236] Central Bank Economic Research: Output, Demand, Productivity, and Relevance. (n.d.). Retrieved July 22, 2015.

[237] Schuetz, J. (n.d.). Why Are Wal-Mart and Target Next-Door Neighbors? Retrieved July 22, 2015.

[238] Dettling, L., & Hsu, J. (n.d.). Returning to the Nest: Debt and Parental Co-residence Among Young Adults. Retrieved July 22, 2015.

[239] Economics Online. (n.d.). Retrieved August 3, 2015, from http://www.economicsonline.co.uk/Managing_the_economy/Aggregate_demand.html

[240] Appreciation Definition | Investopedia. (2003, November 19). Retrieved August 3, 2015, from http://www.investopedia.com/terms/a/appreciation.asp

[241] Baumol, W., & Blinder, A. (2006). *Microeconomics: Principles and policy* (10th ed.). Mason, OH: Thomson/South-Western.

[242] Walstad, W., & Bingham, R. (1993). Glossary. In Study guide to accompany McConnell and Brue twelfth edition economics (p. 480). New York: McGraw-Hill.

[243] Mankiw, N. (2004). Principles of Economics. Instructor's Manual (3rd ed., p. 240). New York: Worth.

[244] Mankiw, N. (2004). Principles of Economics. Instructor's Manual (3rd ed., p. 244). New York: Worth.

[245] Mankiw, N. (2004). Principles of Economics. Instructor's Manual (3rd ed., p. 420). New York: Worth.

[246] Mankiw, N. (2004). Ten Principles of Economics. In Macroeconomics (3rd ed., p. 14). New York: Worth.

[247] Debt-To-Capital Ratio Definition. (2005, September 23). Retrieved July 14, 2015, from http://www.investopedia.com/terms/d/debt-to-capitalratio.asp

[248] Mankiw, N. (2004). Ten Principles of Economics. In Macroeconomics (3rd ed., p. 338). New York: Worth.

[249] Collateral Definition. (2003, November 18). Retrieved July 13, 2015, from http://www.investopedia.com/terms/c/collateral.asp

[250] Mankiw, N. (2004). Ten Principles of Economics. In Macroeconomics (3rd ed., p. 317). New York: Worth.

[251] Karl Marx, "A Contribution to the Critique of Political Economy" contained in the Collected Works of Karl Marx and Frederick Engels: Volume 29 (International Publishers: New York, 1987) p. 269.

[252] Mankiw, N. (2004). Ten Principles of Economics. In Macroeconomics (3rd ed., p. 333). New York: Worth.

[253] What is competition? definition and meaning. (n.d.). Retrieved July 21, 2015.

Endnotes

[254] Mankiw, N. (2004). *Principles of macroeconomics* (3rd ed.). Mason, Ohio: Thomson/South-Western.

[255] Mankiw, N. (2004). Principles of Economics. Instructor's Manual (3rd ed., p. 420). New York: Worth.

[256] Mankiw, N. (2004). Principles of Economics. Instructor's Manual (3rd ed., p. 214). New York: Worth.

[257] Mankiw, N. (2004). Principles of Economics. Instructor's Manual (3rd ed., p.136). New York: Worth

[258] Mankiw, N. (2004). Ten Principles of Economics. In Macroeconomics (3rd ed., p. 335). New York: Worth.

[259] Mankiw, N. (2004). Ten Principles of Economics. In Macroeconomics (3rd ed., p. 307). New York: Worth.

[260] "National Standards for Economic Education." Econedlink. Council for Economic Education, n.d. Web. 27 May 2015. http://www.econedlink.org/economic-standards/national-economic-standards.php

[261] Economics Basics: Supply and Demand | Investopedia. (2003, November 30). Retrieved July 20, 2015, from http://www.investopedia.com/university/economics/economics3.asp

[262] Mankiw, N. (2004). Ten Principles of Economics. In Macroeconomics (3rd ed., p. 336). New York: Worth

[263] Mankiw, N. (2004). Ten Principles of Economics. In Macroeconomics (3rd ed., p. 66). New York: Worth.

[264] Depreciation Definition | Investopedia. (2003, November 25). Retrieved July 21, 2015.

[265] Mankiw, N. (2004). Ten Principles of Economics. In Macroeconomics (3rd ed., p. 427). New York: Worth.

[266] Mankiw, N. (2004). Principles of Economics. Instructor's Manual (3rd ed., p. 231). New York: Worth.

[267] Mankiw, N. (2004). Ten Principles of Economics. In Macroeconomics (3rd ed., p. 344). New York: Worth.

[268] Mankiw, N. (2004). Ten Principles of Economics. In Macroeconomics (3rd ed., p. 292). New York: Worth.

[269] Mankiw, N. (2004). *Principles of macroeconomics* (3rd ed.). Mason, Ohio: Thomson/South-Western.

[270] "National Standards for Economic Education." Econedlink. Council for Economic Education, n.d. Web. 27 May 2015. http://www.econedlink.org/economic-standards/national-economic-standards.php

[271] Walstad, W., & Bingham, R. (1993). Glossary. In Study guide to accompany McConnell and Brue twelfth edition economics (p. 490). New York: McGraw-Hill.

[272] Mankiw, N. (2004). Ten Principles of Economics. In Macroeconomics (3rd ed., p. 5). New York: Worth.

[273] Mankiw, N. (2004). Ten Principles of Economics. In Macroeconomics (3rd ed., p. 90). New York: Worth.

[274] "National Standards for Economic Education." Econedlink. Council for Economic Education, n.d. Web. 27 May 2015.
http://www.econedlink.org/economic-standards/national-economic-standards.php

[275] Mankiw, N. (2004). Ten Principles of Economics. In Macroeconomics (3rd ed., p. 75). New York: Worth.

[276] Mankiw, N. (2004). Ten Principles of Economics. In Macroeconomics (3rd ed., p. 75). New York: Worth.

[277] Mankiw, N. (2004). Ten Principles of Economics. In Macroeconomics (3rd ed., p. 75). New York: Worth.

[278] Madden, T. (2015, July 20). [Personal interview].

[279] Mankiw, N. (2004). Ten Principles of Economics. In Macroeconomics (3rd ed., p. 389-390). New York: Worth.

[280] Mankiw, N. (2004). Ten Principles of Economics. In Macroeconomics (3rd ed., p. 56). New York: Worth.

[281] Starrett, D. A. Economic Externalities.
http://users.ictp.it/~eee/workshops/smr1597/Starrett%20-%20externalities.palfrey.doc

[282] Walstad, W., & Bingham, R. (1993). Glossary. In Study guide to accompany McConnell and Brue twelfth edition economics (p. 490). New York: McGraw-Hill.

[283] Federal Open Market Committee. (n.d.). Retrieved July 14, 2015, from http://www.federalreserve.gov/monetarypolicy/fomc.htm

[284] Mankiw, N. (2004). Ten Principles of Economics. In Macroeconomics (3rd ed., p. 338). New York: Worth.

[285] Mankiw, N. (2004). Ten Principles of Economics. In Macroeconomics (3rd ed., p. 334). New York: Worth.

[286] Mankiw, N. (2004). Principles of Economics. Instructor's Manual (3rd ed., p. 241). New York: Worth.

[287] Financial Market Definition | Investopedia. (2008, April 1). Retrieved July 20, 2015.

[288] Walstad, W., & Bingham, R. (1993). Glossary. In Study guide to accompany McConnell and Brue twelfth edition economics (p. 480). New York: McGraw-Hill.

[289] Mankiw, N. (2004). Ten Principles of Economics. In Macroeconomics (3rd ed., p. 341). New York: Worth.

[290] Free Rider Problem Definition | Investopedia. (2007, May 30). Retrieved August 3, 2015, from http://www.investopedia.com/terms/f/free_rider_problem.asp

[291] Mankiw, N. (2004). Ten Principles of Economics. In Macroeconomics (3rd ed., p. 311). New York: Worth.

[292] Walstad, W., & Bingham, R. (1993). Glossary. In Study guide to accompany McConnell and Brue twelfth edition economics (p. 480). New York: McGraw-Hill.

Endnotes

[293] Full reserve banking. (n.d.). Retrieved from https://www.khanacademy.org/economics-finance-domain/macroeconomics/monetary-system-topic/fractional-reserve-banking-tut/v/full-reserve-banking

[294] Mankiw, N. (2004). Principles of Economics. Instructor's Manual (3rd ed., p. 258). New York: Worth.

[295] Mankiw, N. (2004). Principles of Economics. Instructor's Manual (3rd ed., p. 205). New York: Worth.

[296] Gold Standard. (n.d.). Retrieved June 1, 2015, from http://www.econlib.org/library/Enc/GoldStandard.html

[297] Human Capital. (n.d.). Retrieved July 20, 2015, from http://dictionary.reference.com/browse/human capital

[298] Walstad, W., & Bingham, R. (1993). Glossary. In Study guide to accompany McConnell and Brue twelfth edition economics (p. 490). New York: McGraw-Hill.

[299] Incentive [Def. 1]. (n.d.). Merriam-Webster Online. In Merriam-Webster. Retrieved May 29, 2015, from http://www.merriam-webster.com/dictionary/incentive.

[300] Mankiw, N. (2004). Ten Principles of Economics. In Macroeconomics (3rd ed., p. 56). New York: Worth.

[301] "National Standards for Economic Education." Econedlink. Council for Economic Education, n.d. Web. 27 May 2015. http://www.econedlink.org/economic-standards/national-economic-standards.php

[302] "National Standards for Economic Education." Econedlink. Council for Economic Education, n.d. Web. 27 May 2015. http://www.econedlink.org/economic-standards/national-economic-standards.php

[303] Mankiw, N. (2004). Ten Principles of Economics. In Macroeconomics (3rd ed., p. 12). New York: Worth.

[304] Mankiw, N. (2004). Ten Principles of Economics. In Macroeconomics (3rd ed., p. 360). New York: Worth.

[305] "National Standards for Economic Education." Econedlink. Council for Economic Education, n.d. Web. 27 May 2015. http://www.econedlink.org/economic-standards/national-economic-standards.php

[306] Keynesian Economics Definition | Investopedia. (2003, November 23). Retrieved August 3, 2015, from http://www.investopedia.com/terms/k/keynesianeconomics.asp

[307] Walstad, W., & Bingham, R. (1993). Glossary. In Study guide to accompany McConnell and Brue twelfth edition economics (p. 480). New York: McGraw-Hill.

[308] Walstad, W., & Bingham, R. (1993). Glossary. In Study guide to accompany McConnell and Brue twelfth edition economics (p. 494). New York: McGraw-Hill.

[309] Mankiw, N. (2004). Ten Principles of Economics. In Macroeconomics (3rd ed., p. 305). New York: Worth.

[310] Mankiw, N. (2004). Ten Principles of Economics. In Macroeconomics (3rd ed., p. 66). New York: Worth.

311 Mankiw, N. (2004). Ten Principles of Economics. In Macroeconomics (3rd ed., p. 71). New York: Worth.

312 Baumol, W., & Blinder, A. (1994). Economics: Principles and policy (6th ed., p. 726). San Diego, CA: Harcourt Brace.

313 Mankiw, N. (2004). Ten Principles of Economics. In Macroeconomics (3rd ed., p. 333). New York: Worth.

314 Walstad, W., & Bingham, R. (1993). Glossary. In Study guide to accompany McConnell and Brue twelfth edition economics (p. 495). New York: McGraw-Hill.

315 Walstad, W., & Bingham, R. (1993). Glossary. In Study guide to accompany McConnell and Brue twelfth edition economics (p. 495). New York: McGraw-Hill.

316 Mankiw, N. (2004). Ten Principles of Economics. In Macroeconomics (3rd ed., p. 27). New York: Worth.

317 Sullivan, Arthur; Steven M. Sheffrin (2003), Economics: Principles in action, Upper Saddle River, New Jersey 07458: Pearson Prentice Hall, p. 57, ISBN 0-13-063085-3

318 Toby Madden

319 "National Standards for Economic Education." Econedlink. Council for Economic Education, n.d. Web. 27 May 2015. http://www.econedlink.org/economic-standards/national-economic-standards.php

320 Mankiw, N. (2004). Ten Principles of Economics. In Macroeconomics (3rd ed., p. 9). New York: Worth.

321 Mankiw, N. (2004). Ten Principles of Economics. In Macroeconomics (3rd ed., p. 11). New York: Worth.

322 Mankiw, N. (2004). Ten Principles of Economics. In Macroeconomics (3rd ed., p. 11). New York: Worth.

323 Mankiw, N. (2004). Ten Principles of Economics. In Macroeconomics (3rd ed., p. 338). New York: Worth.

324 Mankiw, N. (2004). Ten Principles of Economics. In Macroeconomics (3rd ed., p. 332). New York: Worth.

325 Walstad, W., & Bingham, R. (1993). Glossary. In Study guide to accompany McConnell and Brue twelfth edition economics (p. 497). New York: McGraw-Hill.

326 Monopsony. (n.d.). Retrieved July 20, 2015, from http://www.economicshelp.org/labour-markets/monopsony/

327 Mankiw, N. (2004). Ten Principles of Economics. In Macroeconomics (3rd ed., p. 27). New York: Worth.

328 Mankiw, N. (2004). Ten Principles of Economics. In Macroeconomics (3rd ed., p. 342). New York: Worth.

329 Mankiw, N. (2004). Ten Principles of Economics. In Macroeconomics (3rd ed., p. 338). New York: Worth.

Endnotes

[330] Joseph, H. (1972). The measurement of moral hazard. Journal of Risk and Insurance, 257-262.

[331] Mankiw, N. (2004). Principles of Economics. Instructor's Manual (3rd ed., p. 204). New York: Worth.

[332] Non-excludability. (n.d.). Retrieved July 20, 2015, from http://www.treasury.govt.nz/publications/research-policy/ppp/2005/05-05/05.htm

[333] Non-rivalrous. (n.d.). Retrieved July 20, 2015, from http://itlaw.wikia.com/wiki/Non-rivalrous

[334] Mankiw, N. (2004). Ten Principles of Economics. In Macroeconomics (3rd ed., p. 68). New York: Worth.

[335] Walstad, W., & Bingham, R. (1993). Glossary. In Study guide to accompany McConnell and Brue twelfth edition economics (p. 499). New York: McGraw-Hill.

[336] Mankiw, N. (2004). Ten Principles of Economics. In Macroeconomics (3rd ed., p. 343). New York: Worth.

[337] Mankiw, N. (2004). Ten Principles of Economics. In Macroeconomics (3rd ed., p. 6). New York: Worth

[338] Mankiw, N. (2004). Principles of Economics. Instructor's Manual (3rd ed., p. 420). New York: Worth.

[339] Mankiw, N. (2004). Principles of Economics. Instructor's Manual (3rd ed., p. 227). New York: Worth.

[340] Mankiw, N. (2004). Principles of Economics. Instructor's Manual (3rd ed., p. 258). New York: Worth.

[341] Mankiw, N. (2004). Principles of Economics. Instructor's Manual (3rd ed., p. 217). New York: Worth.

[342] Mankiw, N. (2004). Ten Principles of Economics. In Macroeconomics (3rd ed., p. 12). New York: Worth.

[343] "Profit Definition." Investopedia. Investopedia, 25 Nov. 2003. Web. 13 July 2015. http://www.investopedia.com/terms/p/profit.asp.

[344] Public Good Definition | Investopedia. (2010, November 8). Retrieved July 20, 2015, from http://www.investopedia.com/terms/p/public-good.asp

[345] Quantitative Easing Definition. (2009, April 12). Retrieved July 14, 2015, from http://www.investopedia.com/terms/q/quantitative-easing.asp

[346] Mankiw, N. (2004). Ten Principles of Economics. In Macroeconomics (3rd ed., p. 65). New York: Worth.

[347] Mankiw, N. (2004). Ten Principles of Economics. In Macroeconomics (3rd ed., p. 71). New York: Worth.

[348] Mankiw, N. (2004). Principles of Economics. Instructor's Manual (3rd ed., p. 204). New York: Worth.

[349] Mankiw, N. (2004). Ten Principles of Economics. In Macroeconomics (3rd ed., p. 427). New York: Worth.

Club Fed

[350] Regulatory Capture Definition | Investopedia. (2010, July 13). Retrieved July 30, 2015, from http://www.investopedia.com/terms/r/regulatory-capture.asp

[351] Walstad, W., & Bingham, R. (1993). Glossary. In Study guide to accompany McConnell and Brue twelfth edition economics (p. 503). New York: McGraw-Hill.

[352] Mankiw, N. (2004). Ten Principles of Economics. In Macroeconomics (3rd ed., p. 340). New York: Worth.

[353] Mankiw, N. (2004). Ten Principles of Economics. In Macroeconomics (3rd ed., p. 341). New York: Worth.

[354] Mankiw, N. (2004). Ten Principles of Economics. In Macroeconomics (3rd ed., p. 343). New York: Worth.

[355] "National Standards for Economic Education." Econedlink. Council for Economic Education, n.d. Web. 27 May 2015. http://www.econedlink.org/economic-standards/national-economic-standards.php

[356] "National Standards for Economic Education." Econedlink. Council for Economic Education, n.d. Web. 27 May 2015. http://www.econedlink.org/economic-standards/national-economic-standards.php

[357] "National Standards for Economic Education." Econedlink. Council for Economic Education, n.d. Web. 27 May 2015. http://www.econedlink.org/economic-standards/national-economic-standards.php

[358] Seigniorage Definition. (2003, November 26). Retrieved July 13, 2015, from http://www.investopedia.com/terms/s/seigniorage.asp

[359] Mankiw, N. (2004). Ten Principles of Economics. In Macroeconomics (3rd ed., p. 76). New York: Worth.

[360] Solvency Definition. (2003, November 26). Retrieved July 13, 2015, from http://www.investopedia.com/terms/s/solvency.asp

[361] Walstad, W., & Bingham, R. (1993). Glossary. In Study guide to accompany McConnell and Brue twelfth edition economics (p. 505). New York: McGraw-Hill.

[362] Mankiw, N. (2004). Principles of Economics. Instructor's Manual (3rd ed., p. 241). New York: Worth.

[363] Mankiw, N. (2004). Ten Principles of Economics. In Macroeconomics (3rd ed., p. 311). New York: Worth

[364] Subprime Loan Definition | Investopedia. (2003, November 26). Retrieved July 20, 2015, from http://www.investopedia.com/terms/s/subprimeloan.asp#ixzz3crbWOiYd

[365] Subsidy [Def. 1]. (n.d.). Merriam-Webster Online. In Merriam-Webster. Retrieved May 29, 2015, from http://www.merriam-webster.com/dictionary/subsidy.

[366] Mankiw, N. (2004). Ten Principles of Economics. In Macroeconomics (3rd ed., p. 69). New York: Worth.

[367] Economics Basics: Supply and Demand | Investopedia. (2003, November 30). Retrieved July 20, 2015, from http://www.investopedia.com/university/economics/economics3.asp

237

Endnotes

[368] Mankiw, N. (2004). Ten Principles of Economics. In Macroeconomics (3rd ed., p. 72). New York: Worth.

[369] Financial Stability Oversight Council. (n.d.). Retrieved May 29, 2015, from http://www.treasury.gov/initiatives/fsoc/designations/Pages/default.aspx

[370] Walstad, W., & Bingham, R. (1993). Glossary. In Study guide to accompany McConnell and Brue twelfth edition economics (p. 506). New York: McGraw-Hill.

[371] "National Standards for Economic Education." Econedlink. Council for Economic Education, n.d. Web. 27 May 2015.

[372] Walstad, W., & Bingham, R. (1993). Glossary. In Study guide to accompany McConnell and Brue twelfth edition economics (p. 507). New York: McGraw-Hill.

[373] Mankiw, N. (2004). Ten Principles of Economics. In Macroeconomics (3rd ed., p. 313). New York: Worth.

[374] Mankiw, N. (2004). Ten Principles of Economics. In Macroeconomics (3rd ed., p. 305). New York: Worth.

[375] Mankiw, N. (2004). Ten Principles of Economics. In Macroeconomics (3rd ed., p. 317). New York: Worth.

[376] What is utility maximization? definition and meaning. (n.d.). Retrieved July 20, 2015.

[377] Mankiw, N. (2004). Ten Principles of Economics. In Macroeconomics (3rd ed., p. 357). New York: Worth.

[378] Walstad, W., & Bingham, R. (1993). Glossary. In Study guide to accompany McConnell and Brue twelfth edition economics (p. 508). New York: McGraw-Hill.

Made in the USA
Middletown, DE
05 December 2016